Decide

— or —

Drift

*THE SIMPLE SYSTEM THAT
MADE ME MILLIONS IN
NETWORK MARKETING*

DENNIS LIGON

Published by Best Seller Publishing®, Pasadena, CA
Best Seller Publishing® is a registered trademark
Printed in the United States of America.

This publication is designed to provide accurate and authoritative information with regard to the subject matter covered. It is sold with the understanding that the publisher is not engaged in rendering legal, accounting, or other professional advice. If legal advice or other expert assistance is required, the services of a competent professional should be sought. The opinions expressed by the authors in this book are not endorsed by Best Seller Publishing® and are the sole responsibility of the author rendering the opinion.

Most Best Seller Publishing® titles are available at special quantity discounts for bulk purchases for sales promotions, premiums, fundraising, and educational use. Special versions or book excerpts can also be created to fit specific needs.

For more information, please write:
Best Seller Publishing®
1346 Walnut Street, #205
Pasadena, CA 91106
or call 1(626) 765 9750
Toll Free: 1(844) 850-3500
Visit us online at: www.BestSellerPublishing.org

Contents

Preface

A few years ago, someone suggested I write a book. It seemed like a preposterous idea at the time, and other than a glorified ego boost, I was not sure why anyone would want to read a book by me. In fact, no one may read this other than my wife, and that's only if I promise to rub her back while she is reading. But what I discovered is I have been blessed with a wonderful roller coaster ride in business. From the time I graduated college as a science major, I ventured off into sales and marketing and eventually ownership of my own business.

During this journey, I made many decisions, some good and some bad, but I also had periods when I delayed making decisions. And I found out that, in many incidences, indecision was worse than making a bad decision.

To give you the framework of why I wrote this book, it was my attempt to help others who are traveling a similar path as I am to make decisions faster and stay on track toward their goals.

For me, I began in direct sales, and through direct sales, earned a seven-figure income. Years later, I began a career in retail through the tanning industry and opened my first tanning resort. Over the years, this grew into a chain of over twenty locations, and I found myself earning a seven-figure income in retail. Finally, I ventured into network marketing and, over the last few years, saw my earnings cross the seven-figure income mark, while working on a part-time basis. The difference in the three industries for me came down to this:

Direct Sales—This requires a self-starting attitude and a confidence in your product and yourself that you can take to the prospect. You have to be the aggressor, in a nice way, but nothing happens till you make it happen. I think probably less than 5 percent of the population enjoy direct sales—so it's definitely a business for the minority.

Retail Sales—This requires discipline, willingness to make the final decision, and also ability to deal with the pressure of possibly losing it all, if you fail. But with proper marketing, you do have the potential customers coming to you. So you eliminate some of the rejection found in direct sales, and if you are willing to pay franchise fees, you can find a model that has worked for others in the past—perhaps giving you a better chance of achieving success.

Network Marketing—Of the three, I found this to be the most fascinating. I know it's a very much maligned industry for good reason. Because cost of entry is next to nothing, anyone can start. However, the failure rate is super high because too many people join, thinking the journey will be easy and the money will flow. Out of the three, I believe network marketing is probably the hardest to build. Why? Well, because of easy entry: many never realize the work required, and once they do, they are out. No one easily quits a franchise on which they have spent $100,000-plus; whereas, if you have only a couple of hundred bucks in a business, it is much easier to walk away. But the big positive in network marketing is not that you can get rich. The positive is that anyone can start, can go at their own pace, can learn from mentors for free, and can do it all part-time. You will surround yourself with positivity and a group of individuals who will lift you up. Although the negative side of network marketing may be the high failure rate and the claims of easy money (which never materializes), the positive of network marketing is that there are thousands, if not tens of thousands, of individuals who have reached financial- and time-freedom through the industry, and who'd had no other options. For them, network marketing was a true game changer.

I wanted to write this book for the people who aspire for a better life for themselves and their families, to show them that any of the three methods I have listed can work—because all three did for me. But if I were advising my children, I would tell them to take a serious look at network marketing. The risk is low, and the rewards can not only be high, but last a lifetime.

In the following pages, you will see glimpses of my journey through business. Mostly it's a collection of stories depicting what moved me along. I do not claim to be the best at any of the three categories, but I know, for the person who has yet to achieve success financially, there are some sound nuggets that can help you on your journey.

The final piece of advice I received that became the tipping point in deciding whether to write this book came in a conversation with a business associate. He asked me whether I played much golf. I told him I was more of a traditional sports guy—loving football, basketball, and baseball—but not much into golf. He then asked me this: "Ok, so let's say you wanted to take up golf, and since you have no experience, we need to find you a teacher to help cut down the learning curve. Would you agree with me that you could probably learn to improve at golf if you had someone to teach you how to hit the ball, what clubs to use, and basically everything you would need to know to be successful? Or would you do better just figuring out how to play yourself, with no help?"

I said, "Of course, I would do better with a teacher or coach."

He then asked, "Would the coach have to be Tiger Woods or could you learn to improve from someone who is able to hit par on the golf course?"

I replied, "I am sure I could learn plenty from the person who shoots par."

"Exactly," he replied. "As long as the individual is better at golf than you, he has something he can teach you, and you can improve. Business is no different. I think you will agree that there are a lot of people who would like to earn a six- or seven-figure income in direct sales, retail sales, and especially network marketing sales. Here you are as an example of how to do it; don't you think they could benefit from your successes and your failures?"

At that moment, I decided to write this book. I no longer worried that I had not achieved the level of success as the all-time greats in direct sales, retail sales, and network marketing. I now would focus on the people who are like I was at the time when I had approached these opportunities. Because I believe network marketing provides the easiest intro to business and also has the greatest potential for success on a part-time basis, I chose to direct this book toward helping those who choose this path. I hope you will find something in this collection of stories that will provide what you need to achieve the level of success you desire.

In this book, I conclude each chapter with three main points: Lessons Learned, Takeaways, and Action Steps. If you invest the time to read this book, please take the time to do the action steps. If I had only one piece of business advice to pass down to my children, it would be to "take action." Fight inertia—get into action. Stir things up. Disrupt. When you get into the arena, things start happening. It won't always be good, but it will be exciting. As the great Teddy Roosevelt so rightly said:

> It is not the critic who counts; . . . The credit belongs to the man who is actually in the arena, whose face is marred by the dust and sweat and blood; who strives valiantly; . . . who at the worst, if he fails, at least fails while daring greatly, so that his place shall never be with those cold and timid souls who neither know victory nor defeat.

Dennis Ligon

Chapter One

Decide or Drift

Y dou can't connect the dots going forward, but looking back, I can see the decision points in my career that had the most powerful effects and led to success. I can also see where indecision led to drifting, wasted time, and eventually, a falling away from my goals. You see, as I look back on this journey, I am able to map out the steps that led to the success I have been fortunate to achieve, while also helping others achieve their success without the pitfalls that had caused me to stumble. This book is a collection of pivotal moments I have gathered along my journey, which led to over a $100 million in sales across three different industries:

- ➤ Direct sales
- ➤ Retail sales
- ➤ Network marketing

What is interesting, and can be a funny thing, is that before I began this journey, I graduated from Gardner-Webb University with a bachelor's degree in science. I had no previous knowledge of business or sales. However, a month after graduation, I made the decision to become a salesman, one who worked solely on commission. My decision was based on an offer I had received from a friend to join in door-to-door insurance sales. I accepted the offer.

If I had focused on the fact that I would be knocking on doors day after day, trying to sell insurance, I would have not even considered it, honestly. However, due to receiving a great presentation of the opportunity, I focused only on the chance to make an incredible income. And a residual one at that. Since it was insurance sales, the company offered renewals on each sale we made. As it was explained to me at the time, we would do a job once (a sales presentation), and if the customer bought, we would be paid a commission. But we would also be paid each year again and again as long as the customer renewed the policy. I thought this was my golden ticket. So I accepted the position and began my career in sales. At the time, I had no idea it would lead to a lifetime career in sales. But the truth behind that statement is, we never really know, now do we? Although I would eventually leave the insurance industry, as you will learn more about as we go on, I would never leave the world of sales, and I learned to treasure always the term *residual income*.

When I got started, however, I recall simply placing my focus on the outcome, the dream, and the income. You might call this the *positive result*. So naturally, I did not spend too much time dwelling on the challenges. And challenges may be a light word to use because, in my case, it meant knocking on doors, commission sales, and no guaranteed income.

I learned a great lesson, though, in what "guaranteed" really means.

You see, friends of mine who worked for companies, and those, overall, who felt they had a safety net with their hourly wage or salary, over time, saw layoffs, terminations, and so on. That was the only guarantee. You are replaceable.

I soon learned that there is no security in the workplace.

The best security is YOUR ability to produce.

Once I was focused on the outcome I wanted to achieve, I just went to work, and over time, learned to develop my skills, until I began to see the realization of the outcome I desired.

In the first few weeks of my career in door-to-door insurance sales, I learned a valuable lesson. I would find myself coming close to making a sale or closing a deal, but in the end, I kept falling short and leaving the house without a sale. You see, in those door-knocking days of approaching people's homes, it was almost like having to win twice. Once, getting in the door and twice, closing a deal. I couldn't figure out what I was doing wrong. Truthfully, there were likely a few things that fell flat for me, but the turning point was a conversation I had with my manager.

This particular day, while talking to my sales manager, I commented about how close I was coming to making a sale. I told him it was like $30 (my commission on a sale) was on the fence; I was trying to pull it over, and my prospect kept pulling it back.

My manager thought for a moment and said, "Dennis, when you start thinking of your client benefiting from your policy, instead of you receiving a commission—you will close more sales." I said I understood, but to be honest, I wasn't quite there yet. Sure, think about the client not the commission—but let's be real, that is easier said than done.

Until, of course . . .

A few months later, I had my first client who used our policy. His name was Glenn, and our company paid him over $18,000. He thanked me for selling him the policy that helped him save his home while he was going through cancer treatment. At that moment, I knew what my manager meant. Seeing the gratitude in Glenn's eyes was worth far more than a commission.

That was a valuable lesson that has stayed with me throughout my entire career. To be honest, *valuable* may not even cover it. I may have to lean on *priceless*. When you truly believe in what you are selling, and you are prepared to do what's best for the client, your customer, even if it means not making a sale, then this will happen.

But understand this, when your motives are to produce the best outcome for your client, it is then that you are the very essence of what a salesperson should be. Because sales is something you do FOR someone, not TO someone.

Try to look at it this way. You cannot connect the dots going forward, only on the way back. Otherwise, how are you connecting them? Sure, they lay the groundwork for the now and the over there—but never for the forward, the then, the future.

Decide or Drift.

The *Decide* side of things is about making the decision that you will take action.

When you *Drift*, it's because you're not taking action. You're in a place of complacency, lazy even. You're not making yes or no decisions. Think about tying that into people's relationships, marriages, careers. There are so many times when people are not making a decision to move forward, or anywhere really. They just sort of stay in the status quo, they get into that comfort zone, and they just sort of . . .

. . . die there.

LESSONS LEARNED: After really looking at patterns in my life where I have drifted, I realized that drifting occurs or can occur many times, because our life has no time clock.

TAKEAWAYS: Most of us have heard that a goal without a deadline is just a dream. So make sure when you are making decisions or setting goals, you establish a deadline for achievement to keep you on track.

ACTION STEPS: Set a goal now, any goal. Put a time frame around that goal and then take action. Like checking a scoreboard on a football game, you will be able to track your progress and see if you achieve your goal when you reach the deadline.

One thing is for sure, when you set goals like this and put priority on your time, you will lessen the chances of drifting. And even if you fall short of your goal, you will find you have made a lot of progress from where you started.

Chapter Two

Pac-Man Left
Me in Major Debt

After several years in the insurance industry, I saw my career take me from salesman all the way to area vice president. Now, what I need you to understand is that this was a pretty big deal, especially to have achieved this level in so short an amount of time.

I became very confident.

Well, perhaps a better word would be cocky. I soon decided I could take a few shortcuts to success. Instead of working eight or nine hours a day, I began to shorten it to seven hours, then six, then five, then to every other day.

To be honest, I had started to fall away from work due to an addiction. Now, you might be thinking to yourself "Wow! I had no idea Dennis was into anything like drugs or alcohol," and you would be right. Because my addiction wasn't to either of those.

What was my drug of choice?

Pac-Man.

I discovered this game at a convenience store and started playing it daily. As I improved, I could play it longer and longer with the same quarter. As ridiculous as it may sound, it became an addiction. You see, when something starts to affect other parts of your life as a result of a dependency on it, that is an addiction. An unhealthy one, without question.

I found myself playing Pac-Man for two to three hours a day, and not even wanting to go to work. Before long, my sales skills began to erode, my performance suffered, and I was faced with being demoted from the area vice president position (that was a big deal, remember?). Of course, I had excuses, and rather than face being demoted or fired, I chose to quit.

That began a period of what I call *drifting* that lasted for approximately two long years. Two years when I would start and stop a job in the course of a month. I went from one job to the next, failing at each one. My confidence continued to erode, till I found myself in deep credit card debt, three months late on rent, and three months late on my car payment. It got so bad that I spent two weeks sleeping in the back of my car just so I could work out of town at a job I had been offered.

When I tell people the story about how Pac-Man left me in major debt, it sounds kind of humorous. But anything you're addicted to, anything that takes your time away from you, can be very detrimental because of the one thing.

Any idea what that one thing is?

You see, we can always create more money, but one thing we can't create more of is time. See, Pac-Man was only costing me one quarter to play, and I could play for hours, literally. But the better I got, the more that quarter ended up costing me because, eventually, I was spending four or five hours playing that yellow-head game instead of earning hundreds of dollars outside in the workforce.

So it was just a spiraling effect that led me deep into debt, all because I made a decision. A conscious decision, one day, to play Pac-Man, and it left me going in the wrong direction.

And for some people it may be alcohol; it may be over- or under-eating. For some people, it may be drugs or something that seems far more serious and far deadlier. However, something as simple as a video game can literally destroy your career. I know this firsthand.

I've seen it happen with people who work for or with me. There are those who fall in love with someone who may not always have their best interests at heart. Or may not want them to work, and as a result of that, they tend to stop showing up for work consistently; then before you know it, their career is gone.

Being cautious and very protective of our time and how we spend it can be so valuable to us. That's why every time I even see a Pac-Man machine or any video game, I'm reminded of a dark time. I realize it's great for entertainment, but for some folks, the better they get at that, the worse they're becoming at building their careers, seizing their opportunities, and retaining their options for earning income.

So Pac-Man left me in major debt, and it's no surprise, given the time I invested in it. And it was an investment—I lost a ton of time and money because of it.

However, out of that downslide, came the most defining moment and turning point of my life.

I could not believe I had gone from being at the top of my insurance company to sleeping in the back of a car. These were the moments when I truly understood what it felt like to have my back against the wall. Breakdown to breakthrough, right? It was in that moment that I made a decision. And I went all in. I went all in on my goals, my dreams, my life, and my purpose.

I prayed, I focused, and I went to work like never before. I was again knocking on doors; I had no choice but to give it all I had. Two weeks later, I had earned more money than I had during the previous six months. I started to feel some of my confidence coming back, and I just kept working. I kept waiting for something bad to happen, but it never did. I kept focused, and over the next year, I earned over $165,000. That was four times more than my biggest year in insurance! The following year? I broke $240,000 and by the third year, I opened my own company. Please understand these numbers aren't here to impress you; in fact, it's quite the opposite. They are to impress upon you what is possible.

During those two years of what you might call struggle, although I lost all my savings, I also lost something else, which can be harder to come by than money. It was my confidence. I had to learn again to respect hard work. Like many people, once I was low on income, I looked for the quick fix. I had a lottery mentality and I just needed one big win. But trust me when I tell you, I didn't want to work for it. I wanted it handed to me. I mean, I was entitled, wasn't I?

And I am sure it won't surprise you that, as I continued to head into this downward spiral, I became a complainer. I blamed everyone else but myself. I took responsibility for nothing. I just felt the world was unfair.

Fortunately (and thankfully!), I was raised by loving and caring parents who taught me lessons aplenty growing up. Teachable ones and positive ones that, above all else, I was never short on. And in case they missed an opportunity to teach me something, I could always count on my big brother—he had a profound effect on me too. Eventually, those lessons my family had taught me growing up took hold. It was then I knew it was up to me to change. Change me. Change my circumstances.

I also leaned heavily on God at this time. I knew my constant bitterness, entitlement, and worry were signs of an ego out of control. I turned the outcome over to God, and I went to work on the things that were within my control.

LESSONS LEARNED: There were a lot of lessons learned from this experience, but the main one was how I had undervalued and, eventually, undermined my past achievements. I really did work hard to grow my skill set and that, combined with a strong work ethic and desire, had led to my success.

Then when I started cutting corners and thinking I no longer had to put in the hard work, but could just make it happen whenever I desired, things fell apart. Success requires a price to be paid. It has been said that "discipline weighs ounces; regrets weigh tons," and I learned that lesson the hard way.

TAKEAWAYS: VALUE YOUR TIME! Yes, you will put in many hours to become a professional, to become elite at something. But you will put in many hours of *focused* time. We tend to put too high a value on money and not high enough a value on time. When you meet someone who is making a million a year and is working a typical forty-hour week, then that means they earn approximately $500 per hour!

As crazy as that sounds, it's true!

Yet some people will treat their time like it's a limitless resource. Time may not be running out—but your time is. We have only a limited number of weeks on this earth. If you start to think of time like most people currently think of money, you will start to realize how truly valuable time is.

IF you could know you were going live to be eighty years old, 4,160 weeks, it might seem like a long time.

IF you are twenty-five years old, you would have 2,860 weeks left; at thirty-five, you'd have 2,340 left.

Now you may still think that is a long time, but if you are thirty-five, you have already lived 1,820 weeks. That seems like a long time too, but was it?

ACTION STEPS: TIME IS RUNNING OUT—MAKE IT COUNT. Plan your week and squeeze the juice out of every hour.

Chapter Three

Little Tweaks, Business Leaps

Little tweaks can make big leaps. I love this because, in building the different businesses, I love digging down and finding small things we can do that can make huge differences. One of those for me was in the insurance business where I was having trouble giving presentations. You see, all my boss heard at the time was that I made, let's say, one sale that day. So all they heard was how many sales.

Then finally, a good manager came to me and said, "Okay, you're selling one a day; instead, you should be selling three a day, and you're selling one. Now, let me hear your presentation."

And so, I gave my presentation, and afterward, he said, "Man, that's good," so he couldn't figure out what I was doing wrong. He rode with me that day, and when we got to the houses, he wanted to see my presentation. I would say to my prospects at the door, "May I join you?" I would look them dead in the eye, and they would say, "No," and they would turn me down, and I would walk away.

My manager trained me to lower my head instead, and then shuffle my feet on the mat in front of me—just shuffle my feet like I'm coming in. Same idea that I was trying to convey with words, but the body language was much different. By breaking that eye contact and taking that little motion of my feet (we're talking twenty-something years ago), that was enough for people to let me in, and so all of a sudden, I was giving three times the number of presentations. I was making three or four sales a day instead of one, and it changed my whole career.

I know that up to that point everybody thought there must have been something wrong with my presentation, or maybe I wasn't working. Well, this guy found out there was a real problem, but it wasn't in the presentation and it wasn't me being lazy, it was what I was saying at the door. it was what I was saying at the door through my body language.

It reminds me of the story of the two men who go to a networking event, and they're just talking to some ladies, and one guys says, after he meets a nice lady, "You know, I was just looking in your eyes. Your eyes can make time stand still." It's so romantic; it sounds kind of cheesy now, but at the time—your eyes make the world stand still, make time stand still—it just seemed wow, very romantic.

Well, his buddy who heard that said, "I'm gonna try it too." So he goes up to a lady and says, "Do you know your face could stop a clock?" Well, of course, he gets slapped.

Of course, the difference is that although both of them referenced time standing still, it's in the way each of them said it that evoked a whole different reaction, right? So the little things, little tweaks that we can make in our presentation or in our training or in the things we offer can make a big difference in our results.

I still remember when we had our tanning business going for a couple of years. This was during the weight-loss craze back in the metabolites and ephedrine days, and we came up with a product that was pretty much a copycat. I looked at what people were doing, and I saw other copycats out there that would sell a product for like twenty dollars, twenty-five dollars a bottle, whatever, and even with paying their staff, they were still making money.

Well, we came along, and we put some carts in the mall, and instead of charging so little, ours was around fifty dollars a bottle; so it wasn't cheap. Now, I was buying this product for like six bucks, so the market was huge; I was ten to one. So you're saying to yourself, "Well, how did you get it?" Well, we didn't get it by selling it for fifty dollars a bottle.

We would ask the lady or the gentleman, "How much weight would you like to lose?"

If they said, "I'd like to lose twenty-five pounds," we'd say, "Well, I'll tell you what, in three months you could do that," and our three-month offer would be $129. We'd say, "So for $129, ninety days from today, you can be rid of those twenty-five pounds," and so, we would sell the result they wanted, and the price wasn't the objective anymore.

If I would have said "This bottle is $50, buy a third one and get it half price, we might not have received the same desired result. By taking the emphasis off the product cost and putting it on how much they were willing to pay for results, all of a sudden, we were receiving the yes decisions, and we made a lot of sales and created a lot of volume and helped people lose a lot of weight.

I want to reiterate, making little tweaks in your presentation, making little tweaks in your training, all these things can make a huge, huge, difference in your bottom line. Same thing goes for traditional business. You see, in the tanning industry, we have so many skews that we can sell; I mean, we sell everything from eyewear to lotions, and there's tons of things. And you can't train your people to be great at all one hundred different items. Thus, you concentrate on the most profitable products, the ones that are going to move the needle the most, because helping your staff get really good at selling eyewear or temporary eyewear that might make you a nickel is not worth spending a lot of time training on those items. You just need you to know what those items are. For example, getting an employee really comfortable on a lotion presentation so that it is very good, where the margins might be two to one or three to one, takes time.

Listen, whatever these are in your business—your biggest profit makers—you want to make sure that you're really good at them and that your team is very strong at them too. No one requires you to be product experts; that's what tools and resources are for—but know the ones that make the most sense to consumers, and know your return on them.

> **LESSONS LEARNED:** For those who have big success in network marketing, it is because they realize that, even though it didn't cost much to start, it is a REAL business. And so, they treat it as such. When you think of it as a real business, you now start to study and look for ways to improve and leverage your time for a bigger impact. Most companies have a game plan for you to follow on how they build their business, as well as steps and strategies on how to spend your time each week.
>
> But for those of you who want to build something special, you will also include additional time each week for personal development. This is taking time to make yourself more valuable. I am sure any professional basketball player is spending time each week practicing with the team. But that player is also in the weight room, eating correctly, practicing on personal time, etc. These athletes are doing what it takes to improve because they know that's how they become elite.

> **TAKEAWAYS:** I've heard it said by Tony Robbins that the chokehold of any business is the owner. The more you improve your skill set, the greater the chance that you can build a successful business. Do a little more than your competition and you will achieve incremental growth. However, if you disrupt everything by taking massive action in your learning and then applying what you learn with action steps, you can achieve geometric growth.

ACTION STEPS: Decide today that "if I am truly committed to this business, then I am committed to become the best I can possibly be." Study mentors who have gone before you, and look for the areas you can tweak that could have the biggest impact on your bottom line.

Then, think outside the box, looking for ways you may be able to disrupt the current model and find a huge breakthrough. But note, breakthroughs usually happen when you are taking action. Don't just sit in a room and study.

Until you apply the knowledge, it is of no value to anyone but yourself. There was supposedly a man who once memorized the entire Bible. I will admit that is an amazing feat, but I can't even remember his name. Now compare him to Rev. Billy Graham, an evangelist who has preached around the world. Billy Graham's preaching affected tens of millions, and he never had to memorize the Bible to touch millions of lives. Increase your knowledge and skills, but make sure you immediately put them to use.

Chapter Four

The "Why" Keeps Us at the State Fair

In network marketing, regardless of which type company you start with, chances are the first question you are going to be hit with answering is the following: what is your *why*? And what I am going to tell you is that you need to decide what your *why* is when you get started. I truly believe it should be done first. This decision, if you will, should take place before you even make a list.

Before you set your goals.

Before anything is probably what I am trying to get across here.

What is your why?

Let me share something with you, and I think it will help you understand more of why I can't stress this point enough. When I was first hit with that question, I remember thinking to myself, "Look I don't care about the *why*. Tell me about the *how*. Tell me what I'm supposed to do to make income." And it probably took me close to a year before I realized the importance of the why.

Let's say you go start a franchise tomorrow. Let's go with Subway. You know, the sub shop. This may cost you somewhere around $100,000–$200,000. It's yours. And you're stuck with that price tag if things don't go well in the first year or two, right? Well, I would bet that you're going to do everything you can to get that business profitable to get your money back. (That was my journey in the tanning business. My start-up cost was $300,000.)

And chances are, in your network marketing business, you got started for a few hundred bucks. Would you agree with me that the drive or willingness to succeed is much different? Of course, it is. Your worst-case scenario is being out a few hundred dollars and gaining the entitlement of saying, "It just wasn't for me." Or the best line may be, "It was a scam."

But I need to speak to you on a serious note right now. If you are not totally clear on why you are doing this business or opportunity, you will quit. Harsh, perhaps—but is this making sense yet? Think of some saying or line to sum up your *why*. And regardless of what you want to call your why, make sure you call it something that will remind you why you made the decision in the first place. It will help you stay connected and plugged in when you go through the downtimes.

Picture this:

You are at the State Fair (county fair, city fair— the whatever-you-call-it fair where you are from). There is a new roller coaster, and not only new, but the largest you have ever seen. It has several loops and areas where you get tilted sideways—we'll call them *swoops*.

You have told everyone that you are headed to the fair and took on the challenge of riding this roller coaster. Your children are with you (nieces, nephews, important little humans in your life). They are so ready to ride this roller coaster. Its shiny silvers and reds are gleaming off the track, which appears black and grey.

You, however, are terrified.

Sweaty.

Gulping air.

But you gave your word to the little ones that you are being a ride warrior with them this particular day. And on this particular ride. How important is your commitment to them? How important is it to you whether you follow through or not?

After all, nothing will happen to you if you back out, so really, you have nothing to lose.

Except maybe, your pride.

And even that is a bit of a stretch.

Ultimately, you have nothing to lose.

And yet, you wait in the line coming up with every reason in your head that you should just back out. Forget it. They'd understand, right?

It's your turn.

Do you get on?

YES! You do get on. Scared, sure—your mind filled with good excuses to not go through with it even. But your commitment to seeing it through is bigger. You don't want to let these young people down, even if it really doesn't mean anything all that much. It, in fact, means more to you than anything tangible. And although the excuses (or reasons) are loud, your why is louder.

———

I have friends who own businesses today that do not make a profit, but they still have three, four, five, six years left on their leases and so, they can't just walk away from those leases. Right? I mean, they would owe that money. It doesn't put them in a position where they could just say, "Well, I guess I tried," and wash their hands of it all.

And neither could I.

When I started our tanning business, not only did I have $300,000 invested, but I had a five-year lease. Meaning this was my commitment—that over the next five years I was going to try to make my money back as quickly as possible. But things don't always go as planned.

Turned out, it took longer than five years for me to do that.

I knew that whether or not I made it back sooner, it didn't matter because I was still on the hook for five years. I wasn't going anywhere for five years. I was committed for that length of time. Hear this again—win, lose, or draw, five years was the minimum to make it work. Now in my case with the tanning business, sure, there would be repercussions if I didn't follow through. I was going to owe that money whether I stuck around or not. You might say, "Well, that $300,000 investment was the why in this case—even with the ups and downs, much like the roller coaster. And to some degree, you might be right— initially anyway. Because let's be honest, money and/or other tangible, monetary things aren't often the driving force in persistence. If that were the case, debt wouldn't be a thing, would it?

I want you to remember this when you start your network marketing business. We all know that you can join and quit on the exact same day. You have to decide "how long of a commitment will I make to this?" For some reason, people lose sight of network marketing being a real, viable business. In fact, it can be as lucrative, if not more so, than a traditional brick-and-mortar business. And yet, even so, network marketing has one of the highest turnover rates in entrepreneurship.

I appreciate there are many variables to this of course. And sometimes, the opportunity isn't what one expected it to be; perhaps the products are no longer beneficial, maybe the corporate structure is a nightmare, and so on. So yes, there may be "just cause" when it comes to leaving your business; however, statistically, people leave because they "don't have the time" or "it's just not working" or "insert excuses you've heard or made here."

And just to qualify, when I refer to "just cause," this could be because your company shut down (it happens), the products or services didn't align with your life principles, you grew apart or away from it, and so on. But these things are typically out of your control—not because things got "too hard" or there was something else "shiny" happening.

So I often tell people when you sign on the dotted line to start a company or you make the decision be involved with a company, commit to making it work. Decide that you will give it one year, two years, three years; whatever you commit to, stick to that. And unless the company falls apart or does something immoral, you stay involved for that one-, two-, or three-year commitment.

After all, you owe it to yourself when the possibilities are amazing. It will be a roller coaster— remember the State Fair? But I can promise you, it's worth every moment of fear, sweat, and all the excuses you find yourself experiencing. Good things happen outside of your comfort zone—and the taste of the fruits are much sweeter when you've worked hard for them.

Find what will keep you hanging in there when things get tough and when you feel quitting is the answer. We call this your why, and it is priceless.

LESSONS LEARNED: I have seen many people say yes to starting their own business. However, what I learned is the commitment level of that yes is different for each individual. This is why knowing someone's reason for starting, or their *why* is so vital.

Some will be happy to earn free product or make a few dollars, and others want full-time income. All parties need to be clear about what they want to achieve, so that they comprehend the work that will be required—because it's quite different pursuing a full-time income versus just obtaining some free product. So before you start your prospect on your journey, be clear on your goals and the *why* that is propelling you forward.

TAKEAWAYS: The hardest lesson I have had to learn over and over and over again is that it doesn't matter how badly I want people to be successful, it is up to them to want it. I can't make someone want to be successful.

I can show them the steps that have worked for myself and others, but I can't make them take any of the steps. They are the ones that have to be willing to do the action. If they are not, then it won't do me any good to beg, plead, argue, or try and push them to success.

It just won't happen until they decide they want it and will pay the price that success demands.

ACTION STEPS: When you have enrolled someone in your business, before they even decide whom to talk to, before they make a list, or get on social media . . .

. . . stop and take some time to decide what they want out of the business, what they are willing to do to get what they want, how many hours will they work, how much time will they give themselves to achieve the level of success they desire.

Do not start going down the road without first knowing the destination and knowing what it will take to get there.

Chapter Five

Capture the Margin

What I should share is that the first traditional company I was part of was when I started my own business; we made photography sales—mainly selling cameras and camera accessories to people who were just starting out. This way, we could offer them financing for high-end cameras and equipment. Only catch was, I had to do this by traveling a lot. I decided to travel to military towns.

Why? Because people are often just starting out in these towns. And despite just starting out, they usually possess a decent, steady income, and the only obstacle for purchasing the camera and/or equipment was the credit.

This was my lesson in margins.

You see, up until this point, I'm not sure I understood this in its entirety. In other words, I managed a team of people and I owned a business. So let's say I would help them get financing—I would earn $400 per sale, and I would be paying my sales people $200. Thus, I would earn the difference. With that difference, I would pay all my expenses—traveling expenses for the team, hotel rooms, major expenses, so to speak. And then I would make the difference. I tell you all that to say this—you better believe I learned really quickly how to use the margins and do whatever I needed to do to make a profit (or at least a better one).

Another important thing to remember is that because it is all commission-based, you learn really quickly how to compound your winners and sell your losers—short and fast, so if someone was costing you money, you didn't waste a lot of time hoping they would get better. Instead, you realized you just had to move on. And when somebody was good, you would make sure you paid them extra bonuses to keep them on your team. The biggest lesson I learned through this experience, even though I earned incredible amounts of money (up to over $1 million a year during this time), was I was not really a "business."

Because it felt just like a Barnum and Bailey Circus; we would be going to a town and working for a couple of weeks, and then we would go to the next town, and so on. There were no real business skills about what I was doing (admittedly), and compared to what I now know about running a business—where we want to get that repeat business and win the customer, and appreciate the lifetime value of a customer—this felt more like a promotion.

So with all of that, and the need to own and run a business—I went to a Jay Abraham seminar. *This* is where I learned more than you can imagine and was fortunate to spend some time with Mr. Abraham, learning a lot of good business advice.

Two of the biggest lessons that made it clear for me were: life is a moving parade and people are silently begging to be lead. Therefore, because this whole business was feeling like a promotion, he taught me how to treat it as such. That yes, Dennis, you're there to make a big sale, get the most you can out of that sale, and ensure that it's good for the customer. Then?

Move on and realize that's it.

The point in all this? Know the difference between a promotion and a business.

LESSONS LEARNED: When building a business, you should be thinking long-term and about the lifetime value of a customer. In a promotion similar to a circus, carnival, or concert—it's a one-time event, where you are just trying to maximize the dollars and then move on to the next promotion.

TAKEAWAYS: Although I loved promotions, I was much more passionate about building a business and building relationships with customers. I prefer thinking of them not as a one-time transaction, but as members, clients, even friends.

ACTION STEPS: Deciding to get involved in the tanning industry, through its retail customer service model, and also in networking and subscription-based companies, where you are held accountable for adding value.

If you continue to add value, then your customer base and your business will continue to grow.

A promotion can get away with a lackluster performance and be on to the next town, but a business must give great value or pretty soon the word gets out and the business suffers to the point that it no longer exists. Bottom line? Add value.

Chapter Six

What Garth Brooks, Eric Church, and Drake Have in Common

The great thing about network marketing for most companies that I've seen is you only have to be good at one thing, and that's promotion.

Promoting the product, promoting the opportunity, and promoting the company.

In other words, you don't have to learn all the intricate things people get caught up in. You don't have to make websites. You don't have to do product studies. You don't have to do research to see what the market wants next with respect to products and things. You don't have to worry about the pay plan. If you buy into what the company offers, then you have only one job, to promote.

It would be as if there were a concert coming, but you wouldn't have to perform as Garth Brooks or Drake or Eric Church; all you'd have to do is sell the tickets. You'd say something like, "Hey, I've got tickets for this concert. If you like this person, here's where you get the tickets," and you'd get a percentage of sales. Well, same thing with network marketing—you just promote the opportunity and the product, and that's all you have to do. Over time, you will get better at that. The better you get at that and the better you get at being able to duplicate that and teach others to do the same thing, the more success.

Once you have that success, you will attract people to you, and the cycle repeats itself. They're going to want to share in your success and want you to teach them how to be successful also.

And then, finally, do what you're paid to do. Yook, you don't have to do thirty or forty things; all you need to do is be a good promoter of your product and opportunity and get better at that.

Consider asking yourself this question: how often is my business open? Because if you're not sharing the opportunity, then your business is closed. And as successful as Starbucks is, tomorrow, if their doors are shut closed and their drive through is closed, they will make no money. Doesn't matter how good they were in the past. They will make no money today unless their doors are open. Make sure your business doors are open by telling your story and letting people get involved with you.

Success and being successful is not about "I've got a good-paying job" because we know companies close every day. It's not about having a great business because we know businesses close every day. Success comes in your ability to produce. So if your company closes down, you don't skip a beat. You know how to produce, and people will buy into you, whenever you add value.

If you want to make money with Drake, Eric Church, and Garth Brooks, instead of spending those twenty years trying to learn how to sing, to write music, to perform, or all these things, become very good at promoting their concerts. For me, if someone says, "Hey, you'll sell tickets to the Garth Brooks show," or says, "Sell tickets to Eric Church, and we're gonna give you a percentage," well, I can do that all day long, especially if I believe in their music and I love it. And I'll be singing it and humming it and having signs of it everywhere, and if you're around me, you'll know I love that artist. I can get real excited about it, saying, "Oh, you gotta go to the concert. It's gonna be amazing!" I can promote the concert, and by doing that, I win as well.

Same thing with your business. You get really, really strong and really, really good at promoting, and that's why the first thing you should see when you're looking at a business is not the money; it's got to be the product and the leadership of that company, because the money, if it's there, hey, great. And if it's not there, if you have to go through some tough times and you don't happen to believe strongly in the product, you're going to have problems.

Sorry to tell you.

So if I'm a big Eric Church fan and have no interest in Drake, I still can sell Drake's tickets and make money. But if he then goes through a little downtime, let's say he has a bad CD that comes out and doesn't do that well, or let's say he's on the downhill for a month or two or a year in his career, then I'm going to have a hard time promoting him because I just don't have my belief in his music. On the other hand, if it's Eric Church, someone I really love, hey, even if he has a bad record, which I don't think is possible, but if he did, I could still overpromote anyway, and say, "Hey, just because that album is not one of your favorites, here are twenty others that you'll love," and I can go on and on and on about something I believe in.

Can't you tell?

You have to believe in the product, you have to believe in the leadership, you have to believe in the company, and then the money. As long as it's a decent pay plan (which if they're competing in this market it should be), the money will be there. As long as your belief and trust in your leadership and company are well-founded, the success will come, and the money will follow.

LESSONS LEARNED: The first lesson is to choose the right company for you. It has to start with a product you believe in. Yes, leadership, pay plan, and company finances are all important in the long run, but if you start with a company because of perceived income and are not passionate about the product, you have virtually no chance at long-term success. Yes, maybe short-term, but never for the long run that leads to residual income. Start with a product you believe in and then do your due diligence on everything else.

TAKEAWAYS: If you have a product you believe in, the selling and recruiting just become far easier. If I were commissioned to sell tickets for the Green Bay Packers or the Alabama Crimson Tide football teams, I could do it all day long. I have been a fan of both since I was about six years old. I would not be dismayed if one hundred people were to tell me no because I am a strong believer in my product and would continue to sell tickets. So start with a product you believe in, and if you promote with 100 percent belief and enthusiasm, you will be well on your way to a successful career.

ACTION STEPS: If you are currently part of a network marketing company, take a pen and paper and write down all the things you love about your product. Make a massive list, and do some self-talk about why you love your product. This should come naturally to you, if you are in the right place.

Now take what you believe, and practice presenting it. You don't have to know everything about your product; just let people know what it has meant to you. If you are believable, and people are convinced your story is legitimate, you will attract the right people to your team.

Don't worry about being an expert on the product; be an expert on what the product has done for you.

Chapter Seven

Health Club Lessons

Throughout this chapter, I want to impress upon you what the insurance company and health club or gym business models taught me, and more than likely, led me to years of success and continued success.

Our brick-and-mortar business is one that we now have in the tanning world, where we sell memberships, which drive a ton of repeat business. And we (my wife, Sue, and I) have our business in the network marketing world, where residual income is powerful too. This is where things get interesting.

Up to this point, I had been perfecting my sales skills and my skills at managing other people to sell well. When I would have ten sales people out there, I would find the person who was doing the best, the one who was getting in the most doors.

Let me explain.

Let's say that I knock on ten doors and get in one. You knock on ten doors and get in five. We are going to find out what you're saying at the door, so we can all duplicate that behavior. Then, we want to see who is closing the most sales, and like the other skill, we are going to copy that behavior.

We slowly would look for the best of the best, continuing to improve our team as a result. The lesson we learned was *testing*—just like most companies do today—we would simply test the presentation.

Test getting in the door. Test every element about the process until we were as strong as we could possibly be.

At this point, it would come down to the talent of the person working. We know this because we had developed this process to a place where everything was equal. We knew exactly what it would take to make money (margins and mindset).

Instead of focusing on the $200 per sale, we got to a different place. Where before I would say, "Your goal is to make $1000 a week," and you would be left thinking, "Yeah, I have to make five sales," we now would narrow it down to knowing we were going to sell one out of every three presentations. This meant you would need to give fifteen presentations to get those five sales, and you probably were going to have to knock on fifty doors to give those fifteen presentations. So your goal was not to make five sales. Instead, your goal was to knock on fifty doors and talk to people. When the end of the day would come, instead of saying, "How many sales did you get?" we would say, "How many doors did you knock on?" meaningful and

That was the big success secret I learned: Don't set some kind of goal based on the sale itself. Set your goals based on an activity that you literally can track and measure.

It was this simple process that led us to build a company, letting us travel around the country and grow the business to a multi-million dollars.

This is what we did up to the early nineties. Then, came the next adventure.

For the first time in my life, we hit big in sales as an independent company—to the tune of my earning up to $1 million as a direct sales person who had an incredible team with my (then) company.

The next phase in my life came in the tanning industry; this was my first taste of the retail world. Because of the birth of my two children, Josh and Jordan, I decided I didn't want to travel anymore, so I opened a tanning business, strictly because I saw a need in the community for it. I realized tanning was so much more expensive in Virginia than it was in California, where I originally was from.

Having seen what was on offer in California, I thought I could do better than what was being done here in Virginia. There were about sixty-plus tanning salons in the area at that time, and so I decided to get down to business. And what is interesting to many is that I never thought about it being my primary business; it was just going to be something I could do on the side. But after five or six years of being in business and then deciding I didn't want to travel anymore, I decided to embrace that business and put myself in the middle of it.

This meant I was going to start building it—like a business. At that time, our company was producing $250,000 to $300,000 a year and making a little bit of a profit. Not much, but it was a great tanning salon environment that my uncle and my brother were running for me. And when I became more involved, we started putting marketing behind it. We started taking everything I had learned up to that point and plugging it in—where it fit.

I continued to receive education on marketing, personal development, advertising—and people. One of the greatest things I learned in business was that when I graduated college with a science degree, that degree was only going to help me so much. But when I spent tens of thousands of dollars on business education through people like Jay Abraham, Tony Robbins, Seth Godin, you name them, that made a difference. I went to them to learn and to constantly improve myself in the sales realm, but even more so, in the marketing side of things. Business is more than just learning to sell.

You see, that's where the tanning business got interesting. I really knew for the first time I no longer had to go find people. Instead, I had to wait for the people to come to me. Most people are not salespersons by nature. So when most people open a franchise, they fear talking to someone, they fear going out of their comfort zone, they look at retail as enabling them to stay in their comfort zones and let people come to them.

The most stressful time you'll ever have is to have $100,000 or $1 million invested into a business, and nobody walks in the door. Ask Blockbuster what that feels like. That's real stress—so the first time in a retail setting, I was no longer going to wait for someone.

I was going out to meet someone, and I was going to decide how many people I wanted to talk to. As a result of my decision, I had to better my skills in marketing. It was like, *do I wait for people at the door?* I've got to get out the message, because understand this, just because you open your door, people don't fly into your place. Especially when there are sixty-plus alternatives.

So the lesson I learned at this stage was BE DIFFERENT. You don't have to be the best; you just have to be different.

We came up with the concept of having a membership. At that time, it'd never been done in the state of Virginia. Memberships had obviously been done with health clubs, and I learned my most valuable lesson by looking not at what other tanning spas were doing, but outside of my industry—seeing what health clubs were doing. And it is here I realized health clubs were offering a monthly membership. I also realized that if everybody who came in the door were to obtain a membership, on any given day, they couldn't possibly handle them all. But they knew the track record. They knew that when a person has a membership that allows working out thirty days a month on average, he or she is going to work out, maybe ten times; some will work out five and some won't even come in.

But the health clubs know what the process is, which allows people to join at a lower rate—thus, producing something different, affordable, and customers who feel they received a good deal. And if they were to use the membership to its fullest—it would be, in fact, a GREAT deal.

We did this in the tanning salon.

So at a time when everyone else was charging $59 a month, back in the nineties, for a monthly tanning package, we came in with a price point of $18.88. Our promotion was basically along the lines of "how could you lose?" It was sixty-something cents a day; people would join, they would get on that automatic membership, and they would stay on. And some people have been on this membership for over twenty-three years, continuing to pay each month whether they came in or not, and that is what we built our business on.

It takes longer, but it works because you open the door to that repeat business. You have to do a good job, first and foremost, and then you have to keep earning that business. But you no longer have to make that sale—you sell it one time, and it continues to pay over and over and over.

This is where we adopted the concept of *client* instead of customer.

You know most people refer to their customers, obviously, as customers. However, if you talk to a professional, you'll hear them speak of their customers as clients. In fact, the dictionary tells us customers are basically parties with whom you do a transfer of goods, a transfer of services. It involves a transaction. Whereas, with a client, you're building a relationship; they're under your care is basically how Webster's defines it. So with a client, you have a lot more invested. You're looking at the lifetime value of the customer (client). Not the $20 or $30 sale you made, but more importantly, that they could be worth $5,000, $10,000, or $20,000 in their customer cycle.

This was a lesson we learned in the tanning world, and in retail overall. We had to learn how to market just to get people in the door, and when they would come in the door, we had to give an offer so different from anything out there that we clearly separated ourselves from those sixty-plus salons. By doing so, fast forwarding twenty-five years later, we now have twenty-five salons, and twenty of those twenty-five are our brand. Meaning, we've expanded from that one location to now owning about 90 percent of the market.

That didn't happen because we had the best tanning beds; it happened because we took care of our customers. Most people fall in love with their beds, fall in love with their walls, fall in love with their name, but we fell in love with our customers.

I believe this is what happened to Blockbuster; they fell in love with their model. They weren't looking at what was happening in the market, and when they had a chance to buy Netflix, for example, they weren't interested. As a result, in the end, they lost it all because they weren't looking at what was best for the customer. So using this example—even though we have a dominant position, right now, in our town, we still look at it as "if an outsider were to come in, how could they beat us? How could they better serve our customers?"

We know we have to constantly up the ante to be better at servicing our customers (clients).

Period.

In the retail end, we learned so much and were getting really good at the marketing side of things. Not to mention, exceptionally good at taking care of our customers. We knew that looking at the lifetime value of our customers, walking in their shoes, selling them what they want, and so on, was key.

We looked at our members to see what kind of beds they like, what kind of services they like, etc. And more importantly, we understood that the customer does not walk in the door knowing what's best for them (usually); they have to be educated to some degree. They might think they know they want this kind of tan, but you have to educate them and show them what's out there.

A lot of times, they'll prefer something they didn't know existed, and a great example of that is the iPod. You see, nobody knew they wanted 1000 songs in their pocket, until Steve Jobs invented the iPod and provided that option. All they wanted was a better CD player or a louder boom box. And someone comes along and changes the whole formula.

This was the same thing in our industry, and any industry really. You are constantly evolving and trying to create something that will keep the customer loyal to you, and which will take that experience up another notch. It's not enough to be just status quo, mediocre, average. You have to constantly reinvent yourself (not your brand, but your marketing, promotions, etc.) and take it to another level. So for me, when it comes to the tanning business, the biggest takeaway was going to memberships and talking to people, letting them see that subscription model.

Today that model is getting even more and more powerful; look at what the Dollar Shave Club did, for example. They went to a subscription model when they found a product that was being overpriced drastically, and they hammered the message of "how could you resist paying three or five dollars a month for a razor when you've been paying twenty dollars in the stores?"

So it was a no-brainer, and it caused three million people, within a few years, to join their membership. This is why, with our tanning business, as I mentioned earlier—when it was $59 a month on average, and I could offer $18.88, the difference was so drastic, it moved people to action. They became my customers, and not just for three or four months during the tanning season—the price was low enough so that they stayed year-round.

And today, subscription models are getting more and more popular because they create a way that you can budget yourself, knowing your subscriptions or memberships will be coming in. In a nut shell? It is a very, very, valuable tool to use in any area of business you may be going into. In retail, that is what led us to seek out more education in marketing—how to get people in the door. It can be a challenge, but when you nail it and get really good at it, that gives you leverage, which, of course, helps you become even more successful.

I want to leave you with a few of my top lessons learned through retail sales, ones that you could start (or should start) implementing, now:

- ➤ Learn how to give a presentation
- ➤ Learn how to get people to trust you (to even let you into their house)
- ➤ Learn how to earn a commission
- ➤ Set an agenda for your day. Time and Money.
- ➤ Budget—it is essential.
- ➤ Determine the amount you need to earn each day.

I used to call that last one the *minimum daily expense*. It was what I had to make each day before I went home. You have to keep yourself on track. Then you learn that it's less about making sales and more about—how many presentations must I get? how many doors must I knock on? how many people do I need to speak to? KNOW those numbers.

It is also about looking outside the industry—what's working for other platforms and how can I apply it to what I have in front of me now?

That is the way you will have success. Build on that process so that, in owning your own business, you aren't realizing you should have looked at expenses a lot closer. And it can't be just about friendship either. I mention this because we know that *warm market* is often a go-to for those starting out. Or in relation to your traditional business, you might like one worker better than another, but that worker may be costing you money and the other one may be doing great.

Relate these examples by the currency each represent. Time or Money. You've got to build your team on who performs, just like they would in professional sports. You can't be too tight in friendships or lose sight of boundaries. You have to be clear that you're here to make a profit, and build your team around the folks better helping build this company.

LESSONS LEARNED: I took a model that worked for health clubs and plugged it in to my tanning business. Our tag was that you either were a Member or a Guest, and we were going to treat both special. But this chapter is a testament to a strategy that made Jay Abraham one of the premier marketing geniuses in the world—the ability to look across different industries to find a solution for your business.

In tanning, we were seasonal, meaning that 75 percent of our members tanned at a tanning salon three months a year. So your average tanning salon made great income for three months, and held on for the other nine. We changed that model with a low-priced membership that would keep our members engaged for twelve months a year. The immediate impact was much less money in the door, but within a few years, the membership (or subscription) model trumped the old model.

From that moment on, any business I was going to be involved with in the future had to have a membership or subscription model. I knew I would give great value to our clients, and if I had a pay structure that would allow me to keep them long term—then I could build my business around my members rather than my products.

TAKEAWAYS: If you are in business, you are involved in sales. Would you rather have one conversation that can lead to a lifetime of sales or that same conversation over and over and over again?

Walmart provides a great example of a transaction business. To get repeat business, the customer must keep coming back, producing another transaction, which involves another conversation. But in a membership/subscription business, now we prove to our customers that we are going to take care of them and they can trust us—and for that, they agree to a business model that allows for continuous payment, like Dollar Shave Club or Netflix.

Everyone wins.

ACTION STEPS: If you are looking for a company or are currently involved with a company, when you are checking out the compensation plan, pay close attention to the pay that comes as you build your customer base.

I am not as concerned about what I get paid on the first sale. I am more concerned that we are adding enough value to the customer that I'll be getting paid on sale one, two, three, four, five, etc. Worry less about the immediate income, and focus more on the residual income, since you know your sale is what you do for someone, and you are going to take care of your customers.

Chapter Eight

Don't Let the Yogurt Distract You

O n occasion, people ask me, "Is it okay to switch companies or quit a company and start it over somewhere else?" Well, that's a good question. I can say that about five or six years into the tanning business, we were reaching profitable numbers, thinking about expanding, when all of a sudden, the yogurt industry exploded here in Virginia.

I mean they were opening up little yogurt shops on every corner and they were making a ton of money. So it was very tempting to go, "Like wow, I'm in this tanning business, we're profitable, we're growing at say a 5–10 percent rate, but here is this yogurt business, and they're growing at a 50–100 percent rate." However, you can't do that when you have thirty to forty tanning beds that you paid for, and all the square footage required in tanning. You can't just flip a switch and jump into another company and start selling yogurt.

I mean, you could, but your profitable margins would start to decline, and you can imagine the can of worms the whole process would start to open. And yet, in network marketing people do that all the time. And companies in network marketing will always go in and out of momentum, just like a stock. They'll be hot one day and not hot the next. That just happens.

What you have to do, if you believe in your product and your company, is stay the course with what you have. You don't change course.

Let that other company gain their momentum; and the people who work for them—congratulate them. Wish them the best, but you stay with what you're doing. Don't jump ship to the hottest thing because I promise you within a year or so, they will not be the hot thing, and that's what happens when people spend their next ten years in and out of different companies and places.

You talk to people who have been into seven, eight, nine companies, and these are people who are halfway successful and they're just taking their teams over and over.

And let's be honest—they're successful to a degree.

Have they made money?

Yes.

But have they built residual income?

No. Because the day you quit a company and publicly announce that you've quit and start somewhere else—guess what? The residual income is gone.

So in our tanning business, which we've grown to about $10 million a year, literally, half that money comes from residual income from our memberships. Take a moment to think about that. That's what keeps me on track, away from trying to go jump and start another business and leave this behind. Because I would be leaving millions each year on the table that would be coming in the door otherwise.

If I were to close my doors and go do something else, that would all go away.

In network marketing, the reason I got involved and the reason a lot of people get involved is the residual income. There is no residual income if you're jumping companies. So the only way you build residual income is over time and by staying the course in the company you're at.

Make that decision about your *why* and the reason you're doing the business; it is, there and then, that you make that commitment. Put time as a factor into your committment, that you will not quit before X date, and really put it out there. Whether it's one, two, three, four, or five years in the future, you're going to give yourself that much time, so you'll know by then that you have a full picture of whether this works or not. Well, we know it works—there are thousands of people worldwide who are proving that theory, but it depends on whether you are prepared to work (and make it work).

Most people, when going to college, are going to spend four years to get a degree. Even if they change course, let's say after three years, they want to do something else, well, they might have to go an extra semester, an extra year. They add time to their education, but they generally don't go three years and give up and quit, not when they're that close. So I would tell you to give yourself time, hit whatever goal you set for yourself, and be committed, unless there's a situation where the company does something wrong or the company closes down, because one thing you have got to realize in network marketing—the reason *why* I've never done it full-time and I always discourage people from going full-time—you don't own the company.

And unless you own the company, you do not make the final decisions.

Putting my whole business career in the hands of someone else who is making those decisions—I don't want to put myself in jeopardy like that. So by doing it part-time, I'm able to make an incredible income, while growing my own business full-time. Alternatively, this is a great arrangement for students, stay at home parents, or those holding a full-time job. Part-time income is powerful.

It's one thing if I make, say, $100,000 in my company, and I work it full-time, but it is another whole thing to say, I make $100,000, and it's a little part-time thing I do, in addition to my full-time business or my full-time job. I always encourage people. I say, get your *why*, and obviously, set your tone for how many years you're going to commit before you hit that quit bell and give up or before you move onto something else.

To take you back a few years, my wife and I, we were earning an income of over $300,000 a year, when something happened to the company and caused it to shut down. Well, if that would have been our full-time careers, we would have seen our income wiped out for six months (the company has since reopened) and literally 90 percent of it wiped out forever. But because it wasn't my sole income, because it was part-time, I was able to continue my regular business that I do full-time and not miss a beat. And eventually, we did launch with another company.

As I said, in the tanning business, we had ups and downs, just like we were talking about with the yogurt shops. There were times when we were struggling, and all of a sudden, the yogurt businesses started popping up everywhere, and it was like, "Wow, they're making more money in the yogurt business.

"Let's go!"

It costs less to open one; maybe I should change horses and move strings and start opening up yogurt shops. Trust me, you start to convince yourself there's no other way. And yet, the grass isn't always greener. Think about Blockbuster for a moment (remember them?!).

If you're in a business, like Blockbuster, that's going bankrupt, yeah, you need to maybe change. For me, in the tanning world, we were still doing fine. It's just we weren't doing as well as yogurt was for a couple of years. So the trouble in real business, traditional business, is that most people would never make a change. Even if they opened up a yogurt shop, it would be something on the sidelines, but they wouldn't shut down all the money and time invested in tanning just to go chase something else, right? Because it wouldn't make sense; they would just try to do better at what they're doing.

But in network marketing, because you invest so little to get started and it often looks shinier over there, one of the hardest things about it is constantly thinking, "Oh, what they've got is a little bit better than what I've got." People tend to want to jump horses, and when you do that, you lose a little bit of credibility each time, and the more you jump, the less credible you become.

And that's where you see people who have fit their whole lives, maybe twenty years in industry, and have joined ten, twelve, fifteen companies. Now they may have made a lot of money, but I promise you, they do not have residual income. They do not have money coming in while they sleep, because they never created it. They chased a paycheck, they chased the immediate money; network marketing is not the best industry to chase immediate money. You'd fit much better in an insurance business, real estate business, direct sales-type business, where the commissions are much higher on the front end.

In network marketing, the commissions are higher on the back end; it's all about leveraging. It's about a lot of us getting a little bit of money, and the bigger it gets, the more that money gets. It's not about making a big, fat check on the initial sale; that's direct sales.

I encourage people, when you're doing network marketing, you've got to stay in the game, and if you've got a reliable company that's been around and has a good track record, because you're taking a chance with it, stay with it.

I've been in the industry long enough now to see this happen. Over the last eight or nine years, I've seen about five or six companies take off, and they were the super shining star. Sad point is that three or four of those companies are no longer even in business. So sometimes things that come too fast, also die fast. Always build on the reliable company, its leadership, and products that you believe in. Stay with what brought you there, the belief level and the things that got you fired up. If they're still holding true, stay there and build—you'll be better off, and you will create residual income that most people would die for.

Timing in your decision-making is everything. It is so crucial in this industry because, if I told you tomorrow that for $500, I would let you open up a new Blockbuster, well, yeah, you could afford $500 maybe, but you'd realize you'd go broke within a month because nobody is going to go to Blockbuster to buy DVDs anymore. Even worse, if I said, "Hey, I've got 10,000 VHS tapes for sale. I'll sell them to you for a dollar each," well, they're no good if you don't have VHS player.

Time and technology change things. Timing is very important because, right now, the timing to open a Blockbuster is horrible (and impossible). Twenty-five years ago, it could have been a great investment, but now, it's no longer an investment. So when you're looking to get into an opportunity, spend the time to make a proper decision.

I say that a lot of people create opportunity. They look at opportunities like they look at a blind date, right? And I always make a joke about anytime when I had a blind date, it was usually over before I knew it was over. I go to the bathroom and I come back, and the waiter is waiting there saying, "Oh, your date has left for the evening, but here's the check," and it ended before I thought it ended.

A lot of people join companies like that. Whatever is shining at that moment—*I'm going to go join this one, then I'll go join this one*—and it's like a blind date that doesn't go anywhere. When you join a company, you want to do your research like it's going to be a marriage—it's a relationship and you're building that relationship. Eventually, when you're all in, you get married, making that decision to commit yourself. You want to have the facts and figures in front of you, you want to know the team you're joining, you want to have confidence in the products, confidence in the company's background, confidence in the owners of the company.

All those factors come into play, especially while you grow larger in the business. Take them seriously, because the more seriously you take your venture in the beginning, treating it like a real business, the better real business results you'll get. Just because you're not investing $100,000 or $200,000, or half a million dollars doesn't mean it's not a real business, okay? You're not going to have to invest the money, but you will have to invest your time, which is even more precious than money.

If I'm going to invest five hours or ten hours or twenty hours a weekend into something extra that I'm going to have to do in addition to my regular career, I want to make sure that it's something I enjoy doing, that I feel confident in, and for me, there is always the *mother test*.

When my mother was alive, when I looked at any product, I would say to myself, "Would I sell it to my mother at this price?" And if I felt like no, I'd be taking advantage of my mother, I would not sell that product—period. If I felt like, "Yep, I would be fine with my mother buying this from me or anyone else at this price, then I would go forward with that product. This lesson can be applied to any industry, and it's never failed me yet.

LESSONS LEARNED: If you are joining a company just to make money, chances are very high you will either fail or move on to another company shortly thereafter. When I see serial company-jumpers, I realize they are not focused on building a residual income.

Even if they are making good money at the onset of the move, they now have lost all their residual income they were building at the company they left. The top reasons most people join a network marketing company are the low start-up cost, the potential to earn residual income that can become quite substantial, and the ability to do this on a part-time basis.

If you are always looking at the next hot company, you will never achieve residual income.

TAKEAWAYS: If the company is solid, and you believe strongly in the product, company, and leadership, then pay your dues. Be the one who leads the company to success. Treat it as a commitment, much like a marriage—*I am here for better or worse.* For some, they jump into a new company like it's a Friday night date, and in a month, they will have moved on to a new Friday night date.

When you commit to a company, the dating is over. It's now time to build the relationship with this company and take laser focus on what you have, instead of what may look special somewhere else.

ACTION STEPS: Focus on what you have at your company now. Emphasize the positive. If you are a start-up, you first emphasize growth and the excitement of being the first, and then, the fact that no one knows you, so everyone will be interested in your story.

If you are in a company that has been around for decades, you emphasize proven track records, the number of success stories, and how your company has proven testimonies of success. Whatever the situation, you bring your talents, time, and desire to the equation and instill your belief into your team and lead them to success.

Chapter Nine

GPS Had My Back

To this day, if I feel I am getting a little lazy, I panic.

Certain things, like clutter in the house, will scare me.

It is a reminder of how I lived my life when I was drifting for two years. So, as you make your success journey, know that there will be times when you may stray off course. But like a GPS, make the correction and get back on track.

Appreciate the grind and that hard work is required. As you go further on your journey, you will come to the realization that it is worth it.

So throughout my journey in direct sales and retail sales, learning all the way, taking education, it was almost funny because in college I was pretty much a C student. Although in my last semester, I became an A student, until then, I was pretty much your very average student, and the reason was all I cared to do was pass the course. I was not passionate about science. I had so many hours in it that I had to stay the course, but I did not want to go to medical school.

I wasn't passionate about science. And I never grew into it either. When it was time for my career decisions, I thought, "Well, I'll be a school teacher and a coach."

I liked coaching, and I thought being able to be a science teacher would probably give me a better chance getting a job being the football coach. So that's what led to getting the bachelor's degree in science, but all through college, I was not motivated. It wasn't a "let me learn this and I can use it later." It was more along the lines of just, "I'm going to learn this and pass the grade and not have to take this course over again."

Now when I got into the real world, especially the tanning business, it was no longer about trying to pass. It was about trying to make money. So whenever I took any kind of courses, whether it was on retail sales, marketing, direct sales, or networking (and I paid money for them), I paid close attention. Primarily because I wanted to learn everything I could, soak up every bit of knowledge I could to go and get better.

I believed and still do, that I would earn more income and create a successful business with the right practical knowledge.

Let's say I am leaving today from Virginia (and I've driven many times from Virginia all the way to California back when I had a business that caused me to travel frequently), and I know it will be around a forty-four-hour trip. When I take off on a Monday, I know that if I drive eleven hours on a Monday, eleven hours on Tuesday, eleven hours on Wednesday, and let's say eight hours on Thursday, I could roll into San Diego about noon on Friday.

However, let's just say I get distracted and want to hang out and watch football with my friends here on a Monday in Virginia, and I say, "You know what? I'll just leave on Tuesday." And then I get distracted on Tuesday. And I would say, "You know, I'm just going to do it hard. I'm going to go Wednesday and drive like fifteen hours, and then Thursday, I'm going to drive another fifteen hours, and then drive, you know, another fifteen hours or so on Friday. I'll get there late Friday night or something." But then all of a sudden, on Wednesday, I get distracted again. Before I know it, I'm getting ready to leave on Thursday—and then realize I can't make it.

That's the problem a lot of people get into in this industry with all its distractions. Whereas, if you have a GPS, if you have a set goal, a set track, a set roadmap that you're going to go on, and you know you want to be there by a certain period of time, you have to set these little points for yourself and for your goals.

In the end, you can find yourself staying on track and realizing really quickly, "Hey, I got off course; let me get back on right away."

LESSONS LEARNED: True goal-setting works. Any sales seminar I attended always included setting goals. You hear it so much that you become numb to it, and the worst part is you end up not doing it. However, if you hope to stay on track and achieve at your highest level, you need a GPS for your business journey.

You can be making a wrong turn with your car, for example, and your GPS will correct you.

Goals work in the same way, when you are committed to them.

TAKEAWAYS: Become acutely aware when you find yourself off track. Remember, there is no failure in getting off track. The failure happens if you stay off track.

All you need do is make that decision to get back on track and start taking the positive steps toward your goals (you know, the ones you will consciously set for yourself!).

ACTION STEPS: It sounds clichéd, but have your goals written down and in front of you at home and office, and even recite them each day.

You need to have them on top of your mind always. Awareness of your goals is imperative— it keeps you on task, so that you can hit them and move on to the next goal.

By taking these steps, you will be pleasantly surprised at what you can achieve over a set amount of time.

Chapter Ten

A Lesson in Sales from the Nightclub

People will join you if they don't feel *sold*. No one likes that feeling. They don't want you selling them. They don't want you going after them. Period. They want to be attracted to you, your posture.

It's just like if you were a single person going to a nightclub. Let's say you're a man and you walk up to six ladies who are sitting at a table. You ask the first one to dance, and she says, "No."

And then, you ask the second one, and she says, "No."

Please do not keep asking until you get to number six. Because I promise you number six is not going to be a happy camper.

You have come across as forward. You've come across as the ultimate salesman in a negative fashion.

However, same scenario, you come into a nightclub or a place where you are meeting someone—your posture is totally different, whether it's church, a club, a golf course, wherever it could be, and now their friends are talking about, "Oh, he's an amazing guy."

This guy is awesome.

Hey, that's a whole different perspective, now that you're attracting people to you as opposed to you chasing them, and you get that by *building your brand.*

What you stand for.

Just like in this book, I could order things like that speech-to-text thing that I bought that I never used. I guess it was a waste of money. But anyways, I thought that I was going to talk on the computer, and it was going to turn into print. (I got sold!) Somebody else, from a place I respect, offered me something else. But what did he pitch?

True story. He came to me and said, "Hey, I have a ghostwriter that could help you finish the book up a lot quicker. I trust her." Now there was no question about what the cost was. And the crazy, funny thing about this is, that's how you get endorsements from people. Solve a problem, the price is not an option.

It doesn't matter. Whether it's $500, $5,000, or $10,000, what matters is I know I need the help, and once I trust the process and believe that you are the person who could help me, I am willing to pay you what you think your services are worth to solve the problem.

It's about solutions.

People will do that, and then based on their result, they will either go forward and do it again, or do something else with those people, if they feel like it was worth the value they paid.

Perception of value is imperative.

That's what's so important—perception of value. Say I needed five ghostwriters, and I put an ad in. In choosing among different people—there's somebody who will do it for five thousand, some for ten thousand, some some two thousand, some for one thousand. Well, that's when you've beaten them on price, and that's a losing game, because the person you get may not do the job.

In my own personal story, what I knew was that someone I respect was telling me the person he had in mind would get the job done. And that's all I needed because of my trust in him. And so, that's why price is not the barrier; the only question is, can this person do the job?

It's the same thing in network marketing. We've had a hard time enrolling people for under $99. These people may not have any faith and belief. They're like, "Well, based on the example of John Doe, he didn't make any money, so I don't know if I want to do this." Before John started, it was easier, and you had people spending $1000 because they said, "Total belief." Once they see John's results aren't positive, they're not going to spend $99.

The point I'm trying to make is, it all pulls together eventually. There are always pieces to the puzzle. Find out why they made that commitment, and you'll know exactly how you're going to place the last part of the puzzle that you put together.

I am not the hero of the story; I am the guy who gets you where you want to be.

And that's what it is all about.

LESSONS LEARNED: We live in a world of skepticism. People are inundated with nonstop commercials. They know that a commercial is designed to sell them something, so when we come at someone sounding like a commercial, we are going to face the same skepticism. However, when we come across as someone providing education on some new product or service, or perhaps we were referred by their friend, they are much more likely to listen to what we have to offer.

TAKEAWAYS: As stated in this book, when we look at sales as something we do *for someone instead of to someone*, we can sleep well at night. If you plan on building a career in this industry, every decision you make is a reflection of your brand. No one sale is worth a dent on your character.

Do what is best for the individual, and in the long run, you will attract success.

ACTION STEPS: Decide what your brand represents. Never chase a marginal sale. Build a reputation that you do what is best for people and your brand is such that if you feel someone is not right for your business, you will pass on the sale and do what's best for them. You may lose a sale or two in the short-term, but you will build a reputation of integrity that will serve you for a long-term career.

Chapter Eleven

Mentor's Story

One of the secrets in network marketing you'll learn from just about any company with which you get involved is your mentor's story. When you start with a company, let's face it, you don't have any history. If I were training you how to handle the tanning business, you may listen to me because I have twenty-five years experience in it, right? However, if I were training you how to run a video store, you probably wouldn't listen to me because I've never done it.

Well, I guess nobody is running them these days, but in any case . . .

If I were telling you how to run a pharmacy or a car dealership, I would have no credibility, so that's where you use your mentor.

Think about the Bible for a moment. Jesus had twelve disciples, and one of them wasn't exactly a good one, but those other eleven spread the word so much it became the largest religion (belief) in the world. We know and practice this as Christianity, and it started with just a small group of dedicated people. Well, they didn't necessarily have powerful stories, but they told His story. They told about this incredible man of God, Jesus, and His story, and the people who bought into that—they became believers.

You apply this thought process: replace this example with your own beliefs, the universe, or what you find meaningful—but I am sharing my story in a way I can relate it to business, belief, and word of mouth.

When I saw the effect that had, one action change, I knew that the biggest leverage I had in business is the marketing, getting people to hear the story, and then perfecting the story, because in network marketing, if you're suffering right now and if you're not having success, it all comes down to one of two things: either you're not talking to people or you're telling your story badly.

A mentor once told me that, "We are only getting paid when we're telling our story. That's when we're working." Everything else we do is sideline. We get paid to tell our story. Whether it's third party, whether it's through a conference call, whether it's one-on-one, whether it's through video. We're paid to tell our story. Since you get paid doing that, you would think you would take the time to craft your story so it's powerful. You do that by letting other people hear it and work it, taking out the fluff and developing it to the point where, wow, it is a powerhouse story.

And you do that just like in writing a book, going through all the stuff you may go through, and then narrowing it down to the key points where you can take action.

Getting that presentation powerful enough to get your point across to people is how you will know that, if your business isn't growing, one of two things is happening—either you're not talking to people or you're telling your story badly. When you're telling the story badly, you're saying things like, "Oh, please join my business. I need to make money, and I think you could be great, and I'll make money." If you tell a terrible story, nobody is getting in. But what I found (even though poor storytelling is one of those two factors at play virtually every time when someone's not making money or having success), nine out of ten times, it's not that they tell their story badly, it's they don't tell their story at all.

When you know you only get paid to tell your story, what if I were to look you in the eye and say, "In the last five days, how many people have you introduced your product, your company to?"

It's amazing how many people I talk to will say, "Nobody. In the last month, no one." They wonder why their business isn't growing. They're hoping someone else is doing something somewhere and making them money. You need to lead the way for your team, and most paid structures are like that these days, where if you don't do any work, you're not going to just leverage off everyone's else's effort.

You're going to have to sort of set the pace and do your part. But if you do your part, you can actually win. So the first thing you want to do is tell your story and tell it well. One of the quickest ways to tell your story well is to tell it often, because the more you do it, the more natural it's going to be. And you can practice.

You can go to your mentors. Let them hear how you're saying it. Ruth Elliott was a mentor of mine when I started in this business. And I had told her I was doing some three-way calls, but not many people were enrolling. So she said, "Well, tell me your story."

And I told her the story that went a little something like this, "Hey, my name is Dennis Ligon. I own a chain of tanning salons. I make over $1 million a year in my traditional business, but I realized that tanning can change overnight. All of a sudden, what's hot now might not be hot five years from now. So I wanted to leverage myself and get into another business, and so I'm doing this sideline business called network marketing."

And I would tell my story. And she said, "Now, Dennis, didn't you tell me one time you were sleeping in your car for two weeks?" And I replied, "Yes, Yes ma'am. That's back in the insurance days." She said, "Yeah, but you were so destitute, and you were out there working, and you believed so strongly in sales or your ability that you started from a low-end."

I said, "Yeah." And she said, "Why don't you tell that story."

I said, "Well, that was long before I got into network marketing."

What she said next *changed everything for me.*

She went on to say, "Yeah, that's part of your story. Because right now, when you're telling your story, you're coming across as a millionaire, and the first thing they're thinking is, 'Well, I'm not a millionaire, so this doesn't relate to me.' But if you tell them that at one time, you were sleeping in the backseat of your car for two weeks. Now everybody relates to you. They're like, whoa, my life might be bad, but I'm not sleeping in the back of my car."

So by making that little change and adding that to the beginning of my story—all of a sudden, I saw my results change drastically.

When you tell your mentor's story, their hero story, that's what gets people excited, because maybe you don't have a story yet that gets people excited the same way. You've been at the company a week, maybe two weeks, or they know you and they realize, "Hey, you don't know anything about this." So you have to leverage the hero.

You have to sit there and say, "Hey, I know you know me, and we hang around, and you know I don't know that much about this product, but let me tell you something you don't know yet. Here's the story I heard. I want you to hear this, and you make a decision for yourself. If it's not for you, great, we're still buddies, we'll still play basketball tomorrow night, but I want you at least to see it. Because here's what's going happen—I'm either going to be successful or fail at this, and you, if you decide to get involved with this, you're going to either succeed or fail. And if I fail, no biggie. But if I succeed, I don't want you ever looking back at me saying, "Why didn't you even give me a chance, Dennis?"

So when I'm talking to people, I give them a chance to say, "Hey, just see if it's for you or not. If it's not for you, no problem. But if it is for you, then I want to help you, just like they're (the hero) helping me." And you use that mentor's story of his or her success and what they've done in that time frame. Then of course, if you have success over time, you become the mentor to others and you can tell your personal story.

It's always better to get that third-party out of the gate—because it's just a better story to tell. It's like I always say, selling and marketing are two different things.

And so, selling—bad selling—would be like the story of a gentleman coming in, seeing five or six ladies, and walking up to them and saying, "Hey, would you like to go out?" Or "You should go out with me for some reason." Well, that comes across as trash; you're selling yourself and probably doing a very bad job of it. (My "Tales from the Nightclub" will help explain this best.)

However, you walk into that room, and those five ladies, who know you, say to the one single lady something like, "Oh my gosh, there's so-and-so; he's the nicest guy, great gentleman. You would love spending time with him. He's so funny; he's this and that."

That is marketing, that's the life you've lived, and it is speaking up for you now; you're letting others tell your story. Like the website, Rotten Tomatoes, it lets people see. I can go there to find people who see movies the way I see them, who like the kind of movies I like, instead of listening to a critic. I just go in there and if I see they like it, chances are I'm going to like the movie, right?

So it's the power of the crowd rather than it just being one individual who likes a certain movie.

So the same thing here. You use the mentor's success and follow that until you become a mentor to others yourself. And use that success story and keep telling that and let the power of that story and how you tell that story be the difference you make.

If I am trying to recruit you for my company right now and I say, "My name is Dennis and I own a chain of tanning salons. We have twenty-one locations, we do $10 million a year and are growing every year. I picked up this little side business and am doing very well at that. I've earned a million dollars." Sounding a lot like I'm bragging, right?

Those could all be facts, but that wouldn't move you to take action, I bet. Instead, what if I said, "Hi, my name is Dennis. My main business is a chain of tanning salons. My wife and I earn have been incredibly blessed of the success we've had with that, but as much success as we've had, and our business has done over $100 million during our careers, we discovered something in network marketing that we believe is going to be even bigger. And why that's so important to me is because there was a time in my life when I was sleeping in my car for two weeks because I was so broke I could not afford the cheapest hotel room in town. I had about a dollar a day to live on, and I was using that for a snack machine. So I went from that all the way to where I'm at today, simply because I saw an idea that worked, and it changed my life forever. What I've come across here, I believe, is just as strong and something that anybody can do."

See the difference?

When I tell that story that way, it has a lot more power than acting like I'm already successful, so big deal. You want to have empathy and be where that person is at.

This helps for those who may already be very successful; you can talk a little bit about your success. But if they're the average person starting out in life, and maybe they have a regular job, or whatever, you want to show them how the greatest thing about this industry is you get a chance to go for big dreams with very little risk. You do not have to quit your job; hold onto that. Then you don't have the financial pressure, but you can still build at your pace, and we're going to be there every step with you to help you build at a faster pace, or whatever pace you may want to go. We're going to run with you as long as you want to run; if you want to walk, we're going to walk with you. We're going be there for you.

Use that kind of a mindset when you're talking to people. Focus on having empathy, and identify with them, and they will be more likely to buy in with you, and move forward with you on their decision.

You know, when people get into this industry, sometimes they have the tendency to think they have to learn a long presentation and they have to speak in front of people, so they put themselves in a place where they really go into learning mode (I call it aggressively getting ready), and they never get started. They're always studying, they're always reading; all that can be good, but that doesn't make you any money. I hope that makes sense to you.

Knowledge has no power until you put it in action.

The great thing about network marketing is what many people miss, and that is it's strictly a promotion business (remember Drake, Garth Brooks and Eric Church?). You don't have to create the products, you don't have to create any of the advertising, you don't have to create any of the materials, any of that stuff. All you have to do is be very good at promoting and empowering people.

We always say in our industry you literally share with somebody a product, share with somebody a sample, then you share with them a tool, something your company has, whether it's a video or whether it's a piece of information on the internet and so on. Then you eventually get them to a leader, get them to a mentor who can tell the story or share the story, whether it's in person, on the phone, or through a video. Let them be the expert.

That is the power of a mentor's story.

LESSONS LEARNED: People are emotionally moved by stories. Many years ago, there was a radio broadcast by legendary broadcaster Paul Harvey called "The Rest of the Story." He would basically tell an interesting story, but it was only at the end when you found out who the story was about. You see, it was always a big surprise.

So in history class, we would learn boring facts, right? Things that would sort of go in one ear and out the other. Sound familiar? But if you listened to Paul Harvey, he would share the same information and yet, it came across as a story you would remember, and more importantly, it would have an impact. That is the same ideology in this business.

Share your mentor's story or someone else's story until you develop your own. But people are almost always moved by "The Hero's Journey." Everyone loves the rags-to-riches stories, and when they are true, you should be sharing them, leveraging them.

TAKEAWAYS: When you get really good at sharing your story, people will begin to see themselves in the circumstances and decide for themselves and come to conclusions like—if they can do it, so can I.

The key is to share it a lot and to make sure you share it well. As Ruth Elliott told me, this is what we get paid to do; it just makes good sense to get really good at what earns you an income. This is what we call an Income-Producing Activity.

ACTION STEPS: Right now, write your story, whether it is yours or your mentor's, and practice it. Get really good at sharing that story, and then start telling it as much as you can. Think of it as swinging to hit a baseball. If you never practice, you can swing a lot, sure, but you will strike out. And if you practice nonstop, but never get in the game, you still will not have success, or at the very least little success.

But if you practice, practice, and practice some more, and then get into the game and keep going back up to the plate and swinging—you will hit your share of home runs.

Chapter Twelve

Somebody

I want you to really think about this next bit carefully. I want to clearly illustrate for you the differences in sales when it comes to one simple message . . .

To and For.

When you're doing something to somebody, then they're an adversary, and that's the old typical "used car salesman" persona that people think of, where you're trying to get over on somebody. But when you're doing something for somebody, you don't mind selling them today and seeing them the next morning, because you know you've made a good decision, made their life better. It was the right product for them.

If you approach sales like that, you'll always sleep well at night, feel good about what you did, and really be confident and proud of your product and your company.

When I see people who do not want to talk to their family and friends in network marketing, what that tells you is quite a few things. They have a past that they don't want to follow them the way they live their lives. But a lot of the time, they don't have 100 percent belief in their product. And they don't want to be the person to talk someone into something that they don't believe in. Because if they're really passionate about it, I would say that 90 percent of all their sales will not need any kind of closing technique—as long as they have 100 percent enthusiasm and belief.

When you're in the third grade, you're not going to understand algebra, but you're learning math, and one day, you're going to learn algebra. And it's step by step by step.

> **LESSONS LEARNED:** When building a business, and one that values the customer or client over the product, you are always looking for what's best for your customer, client, or prospect.
>
> When you approach selling TO A CUSTOMER, you are thinking of your own gain. As a friend of mine, John Melton, once said, "They can smell your commission breath."
>
> When you approach selling FOR THE CUSTOMER, and you truly are being ethically solid, you will build trust. And with that trust, you can build a successful career and help a lot of people in the process.

> **TAKEAWAYS:** When you decide to build your brand, you will not fall prey to pursuing the quick sale. Most people who fall guilty to trying to make the quick hustle find themselves desperate for a sale or to enroll someone in their business. Because they do not have a foundation for their business, they are always in reactive mode and trying for that quick fix. When you DECIDE what your brand is about and approach every sale or enrollment based on the culture of your brand, you will not be tempted to sell a product to someone who does not need it or to pressure someone to start a business that they are not certain about. You want to build a long-term, ethical business, and

THIS is your brand— so start with honesty and integrity, and build from there.

ACTION STEPS: Do a quick check of your motivations. When you are talking to someone, are you listening to what they are telling you or are you waiting for them to stop talking so you can go back to selling to them again.

Once you are clear in your head that your motivation is to do what is best for your prospect, a solid, successful business is the only outcome.

Chapter Thirteen

Timing is Everything

Given the variables of this industry—I knew before I put my entire business career in the hands of someone else who would be making the final decisions, I didn't want to put myself in jeopardy like that.

So I knew that by doing the network marketing business part-time, I would be able to make an incredible income, and I promise you that this is a great highlight when you're trying to prospect and recruit other people.

You see, it's one thing to say, "I earn $100,000 a year in my company and I work it full-time," but it is an entirely different thing to say, "I earn $100,000 a year in my company and it's a little part-time thing I do, in addition to my full-time business or my full-time job."

That is when it really carries some weight because now we're talking an *extra* or *additional* income—not the entirety.

My wife and I, we were making an income of over $300,000 a year at one point in network marketing, and unfortunately, some things happened to that company and caused it to shut down temporarily. Sure, it's back open for business now, but at a fraction of what it was back when we were involved.

Well, if that would have been my full-time career I would have seen my income wiped out for six months.

And literally 90% of it wiped out forever.

But because it was part-time, I was able to continue to build my regular business that I do full-time and not miss a beat. Eventually, we decided to launch another company—but never wavered from the power of part-time.

You see, this is why I always caution people about doing this industry full-time. You never know, and given, you don't always know with jobs either— but having this income as an additional stream is a great way to bank extra money, and at the very least, it gives you options.

My best advice when someone's looking at network marketing or getting started is all about your *why*. Build a strong part-time business throughout the process, and I would recommend that you do not go full-time. Unless of course you are making so much money that it's insane not to go full-time—on average? A minimum of $20,000 per month and have at least six months banked (just in case).

Now that we have that covered—it was important for me that this be included because I appreciate people want to dream big, myself included, but calculated risks are important. This can be such a powerful vehicle, when done right, and can be devastating if something happens that you have no control over.

Now let me circle back here for a moment to the company vs. you. This may come across as a dualism, but I promise you it is not at all.

You are excited, your company has a ton of great marketing materials and goodies for you to share—great! I would guess that this creates a great situation for you to brand that company and spread their name. However, who exactly is this great for? Again, this isn't to suggest that you should never use your company-branded content— but make sure *who you are* outweighs that, especially on social media and things of that nature.

This is important for a couple of reasons: People join people, not companies.

Your company may not always, align with what you are hoping to attract. I promise you, everybody who owns a Subway franchise never dreamed Jared would end up getting arrested and going to prison, right? What a nasty mark that put on the brand that had been using him as their extension of the brand. Everybody knows the Jared story, right?

So it's very important when you do build the business part-time that you focus on branding *you*. The same can be said about those who build their business full-time—however, chances are they have (you) have those strategies figured out by now. This message is more so for those who were "sold" on the opportunity to work for themselves, full-time.

Remember, when people join a company, based on what they have to offer—there is little loyalty to you. However, we have learned first-hand that this is, in fact, a people business, a relationship and attraction marketing world, so give "your people" something to stick around for.

Give them a cause, a culture, and a purpose to plug into.

And remember how much more powerful $100K a year part-time sounds versus $100K a year full-time. Please also note that whether it be full-time or part-time—to achieve those levels of income numbers, these are from people building businesses, not hobbies.

LESSONS LEARNED: When I got into network marketing, I treated the company like I was the owner. Eventually this backfired on me when the company faced some hardship due to regulations and had to enter into a court battle.

When you join a network marketing company, you are building your own business within that company. So you definitely want to pick a company that you are passionate about. And if you are a serious builder in said company, you realize people are buying into you and what you bring to the table.

What differentiates you from any other distributor? Why would anyone join you? That's the question you should ask yourself. Every day, seek to get better and better at building your personal brand.

You promote the company's products and opportunity, but you lead with your personal brand. In the beginning, you may not feel you have that much to offer, but as long as you are there for your team and help direct them to success, that will be enough for them to develop trust in you and take the journey with you.

TAKEAWAYS: The most important attribute about your personal brand will be integrity. When a survey was done of decamillionaires (individuals with over $10 million in net worth), the most common ingredient that was instrumental in all of their successes was integrity.

To grow a successful business and a successful team, you will need integrity, no question about it. So make it the cornerstone of your business, and you will attract people with the same qualities—and integrity.

ACTION STEPS: Before you recruit the next person or sell to the next customer, answer this question: What does my business stand for?

If someone were to ask you today what makes you different than someone else with whom they could enroll, what would you say? Let people know what you offer, and as your success grows, your story will grow as well.

A good beginning place for me, and what I would say is this: "As long as you are willing to do what it takes to be successful, I will be there with you. I will never give up on you, even if you give up. I will give you 100 percent of everything I have, and I am committed to your success."

Chapter Fourteen

Learn + Pass

Y ou know, the surprising thing is (well, to me anyway) when I went to college, it was because that's what I was expected to do. I got into college, and was kind of surprised that I did; but I got into a small college and I did okay, but it was funny—I didn't have any kind of powerful why.

I was just going through the motions and knew I had to pass the classes just like I did in high school or elementary school or middle school. It was just something that you knew you were required to do. But I didn't have any passion to learn science, which was my major.

And it wasn't until my senior year, when I had to deliver the check for my tuition (My mom had not mailed it in, and so my mom and dad had me deliver it) and I looked into the envelope and saw the amount of the check (I was nosey, I admit it), that it really dawned on me how much of an investment they were making in my college education.

I don't know what I was thinking beforehand, but when I saw that, I got serious, and that senior year is when I had an A year. That's when I had close to a 4.0 for the whole year because I was taking it seriously; whereas, up until then, I hadn't been.

So that's where the power of the why comes in when you're doing your business. During college, I simply had no why whatsoever; it was just "pass the grades" because that was what I was expected to do. I wasn't a very motivated student; but when I got down to business and had a powerful why and wanted to achieve, that's when I started realizing successes.

You know, it was funny. I was the same guy who was barely making it in college, and yet, ended up the last year in college doing well. I was the same guy who achieved success in insurance, and who then failed miserably by playing video games. So though it's the same person, it's just the actions you take and the habits you develop that make all difference in the world. The difference being whether you're going to decide to make an impact or you're going to drift along and let the days pass by.

LESSONS LEARNED: This short chapter carries a very important message. What is your true motivation? Why did I barely get by in college? Well, because I had no idea why I was even there, except to pass. Not a big motivator. To achieve big, you have to have a big reason for what you are doing, or you may find yourself settling for average results.

TAKEAWAYS: Once you are inspired by a WHY, a reason why you must make something happen, you are hard to beat. Now you go from average to amazing at the speed of thought. As stated before, Thoughts are Things. Now you have a reason to be excellent and you will find an inner drive that didn't exist before.

ACTION STEPS: I have heard the story several different ways, but in one version, a pedestrian is walking by two construction workers who are laying bricks on a wall. The passerby asks the first worker, who seems to be miserable as he is going through his task, what he is doing? The construction worker replies, "Laying bricks for thirteen dollars an hour." The pedestrian walks over to the second construction worker, who seems excited, and asks him what he is doing. The second construction worker says, "I am building a cathedral!"

Both workers had the same task for the same pay, and yet, one was inspired by his Why, and that made all the difference in how he viewed his job.

Chapter Fifteen

Love on Other People

How about positioning the brand itself? Whether you're selling a product, or whether you're starting a business and getting someone to enroll in your business or buy your product, it all starts with *not* putting the emphasis on you or on your product or on your success, which is what a lot of people do.

For instance, in the tanning world, they'll talk about, "Hey, we've got the best tanning beds, we've got this, that, this and that." There's a place for that, but most importantly, the message to your customer should be, "What's it going to mean to you?"

In other words, if Teresa comes into our tanning spa, how is her life going to be different by using our services? Our message should be, "Love yourself and treat yourself to our service." It's all about Teresa. She's going to be more confident. More self-assured. You know, feel more attractive, after spending a little time in our place. That's the one thing we care about. Teresa doesn't really care how great our beds are; she cares about how she's going to look afterwards.

Same thing with a trainer. You've got a trainer with a lot of great equipment, but if another trainer says, "I can get you in the best shape of your life in thirty days," that's the person you're going to go to, regardless of what kind of equipment he has.

One of the major mistakes people make in the network marketing industry or in the direct sales industry is they put all the emphasis on their products, the features, maybe the benefits of the products; they need to totally turn that around.

It needs to be about the person.

In my experience, empathy—getting into the customers' shoes, seeing what they're looking at and their aspects—go a long way. And once they realize they can do what you are doing too, chances are they're getting in the business. If there's any doubt, it doesn't matter how much money everybody else has made; if they cannot see themselves doing the activity required to make money, they're going to say no every time.

Network marketing has always been very good about seeing people as they could be, instead of as they are right now. They may be used to going to a job, getting paid wages for doing a certain amount of work, yet, there was no recognition that came with that. It's like "here's your ten bucks for the job you did; that's what you we're trading your time for, this money." And in network marketing, before the money got there, they realized really quickly that people will do a lot more for recognition than they will for money. And so, the recognition was pretty heavy.

You know people will move mountains for that recognition. And so, that's one thing that network marketing has done so well, make sure people get a lot of recognition for their achievements, number one, and then number two, future pace into thinking what's possible to keep them dreaming, keeping that carrot out there, so to speak.

You are getting them to think of the future, as opposed to where their situation is right now. You're getting them to dream a lot bigger than their current situation, using network marketing as the vehicle to get there. One thing people can take away from network marketing and direct sales, or anything that's commissioned-based, is recognition.

Loving on people, making them feel good, talking faith into them, getting them to believe bigger in themselves.

Positive reinforcement and a lot of recognition, as opposed to always just telling people what they do wrong, or not recognizing them at all—goes ten times further.

I had several managers in the tanning business who were famous for leaving notes every day on Post-its, telling staff what they did wrong the night before. Pretty much, it just sets such a sour tone, right? We had people quitting or wanting the manager fired. When really, all the manager had to do was just sit down, face to face, and tell the person, "Hey you did this great; here are some mistakes here that you need to correct, but love having you work here."

Do the "ole sandwich" approach; tell them what they're doing great, tell them what the problem is that you're really having to address, and then end it up with, "Hey, I believe in you, and you straighten this little thing out, and we'll go from there; but great things are ahead."

Loyalty, Loyalty, Loyalty

When you build the company's brand, then those who join your team and choose to work with you are going to be loyal to that company's brand. Seems like a bold statement, but it's true. You see, you sold them on the company concept—not on who you are.

Don't get me wrong, it's okay for them to be loyal to the product or the brand of that company, but you want them loyal to you. You want people loyal to what you're teaching and what you're bringing to the equation.

So the next action step is, once you've got your *why*, once you've committed that you're not going to quit before your goals and efforts match—you're going to give it 100 percent to have success. Then, as you're following the policy of your company, and that is whatever company you're working for (with), it is very important that you start establishing yourself as a brand.

Time to show people what you're bringing to the table. It's always fascinating to me that when people go out and recruit someone in network marketing, and they want you to join you, well . . . you'd better have something to bring to the table. Instead of something like, come join me I want to make more money.

That's not going to do it. In fact, I think you will agree it will have the opposite effect or result that you are looking for.

When you focus on building your brand using the steps above, then, if you ever have to go to another company or anything drastically changes, people will not just forget about you—they will literally follow you, if you've done a good job of leading.

And that is fact.

LESSONS LEARNED: When you begin your career you are in hopes that your company will be around forever. When most people join a network marketing company their main thoughts are, "Can I do this? How long will it take for me to make my investment back? How much money can I earn?" The one question they rarely ask is, "Will this company ever go out of business?"

But network marketing companies fail just like retailers do. There is no guarantee that the company you choose will be around forever. So since you will be investing considerable amounts of time and capital building a team, make sure you build a team that is loyal to you, as well as the company.

This means making sure you are in consistent contact with your team and know all of their contact info: email, mobile numbers, address, etc. If the unthinkable were to happen one day, with your company shutting its doors, the team may be willing to follow you to another opportunity, if that were your only option, but only if they still respect your leadership.

TAKEAWAYS: Understand that no business is bulletproof. Businesses that seemed too big to fail twenty years ago are now just a memory. Work each day believing your company will be around forever, but always take the necessary steps to be prepared in case it all were to end tomorrow. Planning is key. And how you treat others is the determining factor about what happens next.

ACTION STEPS: Go through the people on your team and make sure you have all contact info. If something were to happen tomorrow, how many of your team could you reach? The time to prepare for a crisis is before the crisis.

We hope and believe it will never happen, but if it does, you will be prepared.

Chapter Sixteen

Momma's Lesson

I watch Eric Worre, who is a fixture in this industry. I see him as one of the most successful coaches, earning who knows how much income, but to the tune of multimillions through the programs he puts on.

The first year I followed him, it was all free content he delivered, and over delivered. Every few days, he had a free video for four or five minutes telling you tips on network marketing, and I thought, "This guy's good, but he must not be too smart because he's giving all this stuff away."

And then finally, a year goes by and he hosts a little seminar where about 300 people attend—they all purchase a ticket around $99 (or something) for training. And I watch him grow and grow some more. After about five, six, seven years of doing this, he's now having seminars that people are paying up to $300 to attend, and 15,000 people show up. He does private coaching, plus he has other seminars, and he does this around the world.

I share all that, to say this: He created a multimillion dollar legacy—I mean huge, huge business all starting from simply offering stuff for free the first year.

Meanwhile, he built his list.

He built his database, but before he was asking you to spend any money with him, the motive was "I'm going to give you value first."

And it's the same thing with writing this book or in a website. For me, it's following that design and taking the things I have learned from others and the things I have learned from the traditional business world and my direct sales experience—taking all that, wrapped up, and sharing that with people.

This will not only shorten the learning curve for you (and others) but it will help create great success, because as exciting, as fun, as enjoyable, and as big a thrill as it was creating my own success and feeling the joy of the rewards of that . . .

It pales whenever you're able to help someone else.

I promise you.

I remember Mom, when we were little, said to me, "It's better to give than to receive."

I said, "Well, Momma, I'm glad you feel that way, but I'll be on the receiving end. If you keep giving, I'll keep receiving."

But I learned later on how true was her message, when I saw people I'd helped earn $100,000, $200,000, get a new car, get a new house, all because I took the time to work with them. And it was then that they used their own talents and their own successes, and they achieved, and I just sort of played a little part in that.

That was a greater reward for me than anything I've achieved for myself, personally.

So understand you can do the exact same thing. There are plenty more who have done a lot more than I have. But it's simply a great industry, where you're able to help yourself by helping others.

I like to think that network marketing, done in the right way, is truly the golden rule in action.

LESSONS LEARNED: Your greatest security is in your ability to produce. No company can give you security. Companies close each year, but you secure your future by what you are able to do. You will always attract people, if you add value. As my mother taught me, and as so many of you have been taught, it is better to give than to receive.

If you begin your career by looking for ways to give, give, and give without worrying about what you get back, you will build a culture and build a successful team that will follow you anywhere.

TAKEAWAYS: This is such an easy differentiator. There is such a mass of people starting a network marketing business focused on what they can get, what can the company do for me, and trying to recruit others with the sole thought of how much money those recruits can make for them.

If you take the opposite approach and think of recruiting people who you can pour value into, you will set yourself apart from most people trying to build a business.

You will rise to the top by placing your focus on others' success.

ACTION STEPS: What can you do today to make this business simpler and more doable for your team? Can you call and encourage someone today? Can you do a three-way call for someone, or FaceTime with a prospect?

Do something to let your team know they are your top priority, and that when you recruited them into the company, that was the day your work really started.

Spend the time growing your people, and one day, your people will grow your business.

Chapter Seventeen

NFL and Your Commercial Break

W hen writing this book, I came to realize it was more about connecting the dots than anything. You know, you can't connect the dots going forward, you can only connect them looking back. And if you can train yourself to make better decisions, faster—instead of drifting between decision to decision—you will find your results will happen faster, and you'll get better results.

I say all that, to say this: the whole point I've learned in going through my life is that what it took me twenty, thirty years to achieve could have been done a lot quicker, if I were able to take away all those drifting moments, as I call them.

You know, it's funny, I looked at an NFL football game. Work with me here—a football game that you watch on TV, think about it.

A game will last you probably about three hours, three hours and fifteen minutes, by the time they do all the commercials, the time-outs, the half-times, the quarters, all that stuff, right?

The actual game itself, as we know, lasts sixty minutes, okay?

So that sixty minutes is being stretched out to three hours. But what's even funnier is the actual play, when something is actually happening, is I think roughly around eight or nine minutes of actual action. Because they have a play that takes about ten seconds and then they go and huddle for forty-five seconds. Next whistle, they have a play lasting about eight seconds and then they go huddle for like forty seconds. And so, it's almost as though, more than anything, you're looking at a huddle. Or you're looking at replays or you're looking at people talking or you're looking at commercials. Right?

So in that context, the world of football has learned they can take eight or nine minutes of action and create a three-hour program for which people will pay or sit and watch three hours' worth of commercials and everything else that goes with it.

If they were to stretch it out too far though, with too many time-outs, too much talk at half-time, or simply going too long, eventually people would lose interest and they wouldn't stay a part of it.

So, what's important about that is this: as you're going through your career, you have that deadline, that goal that you want to get to, and you set little deadlines for yourself. But whether you hit them or miss them, it's a matter of keeping yourself on track. And when you get off track or drift off, which you always will from time to time, it is having set points where you get yourself back on track and back into action.

Because this industry will bring you lots of huddle time. There will be small glimpses of action here and there—even some big wins along the way too. But to get to them, and to keep yourself interested as well as those you are engaging—you need to find love and passion for it in the down times too.

LESSONS LEARNED: Many times people start a business loaded with enthusiasm. It's like the start of a marathon (okay, I have never run, so this is the way it looks to me), there is so much enthusiasm from the runners.

At the end of the marathon, there is also much enthusiasm from the crowd and a sense of accomplishment from the runners. However, during the twenty-plus miles, there is a long stretch of no crowds, no cheers, so you better be prepared to be motivated from the inside. In business, like in a football game, there will be moments of exhilaration, but there will be many more mundane moments. In other words, be certain of what you are trying to accomplish and that you are there through it all.

TAKEAWAYS: Like an athlete who appreciates practice—I had no problem with the day-to-day tasks of business, because I felt the endgame was worth it. To experience the success of a task well done was worth it to keep going.

A thermometer can tell you the temperature of the room, but a thermostat sets the temperature of the room. When I got into business, I relished being the thermostat.

ACTION STEPS: Now that you have started, and make sure you have STARTED, prepare to make the most of your working hours. Preparation, similar to that of an athlete, and growth of your skill set will increase your odds for success.

Business is not a game of luck. In fact, there are actions you can do to increase your chances of success. Do not leave it up to others to decide your fate. You set the temperature of the room. You are the thermostat of your business. Take the steps today to move forward and leave your business better off today than it was yesterday.

Chapter Eighteen

What the Backseat of My Car Taught Me, and How It May Inspire You

M ight not be the story you were expecting here . . . but I think you will enjoy it anyways.

The backseat of a car: it's very humbling to think I was there at one time and to think about when you're in the backseat of a car and you're looking up, you know, back in those days, looking up through the window and you're seeing the stars above you, you do a lot of soul searching, you do a lot of praying.

But the funny thing about being in the backseat of that car, the second night I was there was after I had made three or four sales from working in that area. And every night, I was in the backseat of the car looking up and staring at the stars. You would think I would have been depressed, crying, how can my life get like this? But instead, every night I was there, I was fired up, except for the day when I went by the little service station and hit the snack machine and it didn't throw out my snack. This might sound trivial to you, but I had only a dollar a day to spend. And I put a quarter in there for my drink, 35 cents for a snack (it might have been a honey bun; it was probably something that wasn't good for me anyway), but it did not fall through. It got hung up and I about felt like I was going to rock that machine off its axis. I just wanted that snack so badly because I didn't have any other money to buy something to eat or drink.

But aside from that, I went to bed every night very peacefully and slept in the backseat of that car because all of a sudden, I saw my life turning around. Every day my confidence got better because that very first week, during which I slept in the backseat of my car, I earned $1,500. The year prior, I had made only about $8,800. That was the year I had been more broke than ever. It was where I lost it all.

But the backseat of that car was humbling. It was as though it helped keep me grounded this time around.

One week, I earned $1,500, the next week I earned $1,800, and from that point on, I was earning about $3,000-plus each week. That year I earned $165,000. So to go from $8,000 to $165,000 a year, that is a paradigm shift, for sure. But it happened when I was in the backseat of a car.

Why would that be?

What should have been the most depressing point in my life turned out to be one of the most exciting, at least in regard to business and financial matters. And I believe it is because that's when my confidence came back; that's when I went from feeling like a loser who couldn't do anything to now feeling like a champion.

And every day, it got better and better, and I kept thinking that one day, I would tell this story, and here, all these years later, I've told this story so many times. So, what I saw was that a story so bitter and disappointing, at the time, became the story that really launched my career. It was this experience that kept me going all these years later because it has kept me on track.

I know why I ended up there.

It wasn't because I had a drinking problem or some serious addiction, it was literally goofing off, being lazy, drifting, playing Pac-Man, doing useless things, wasting my time, and so on. It took me until that point to realize, "You've wasted time long enough; your confidence is going down. Not only do you not want to sell, you no longer believe you can sell." When you're living in the backseat of a car, your back is against the wall and you gotta try. And thank God, that first night, I made sales, and that took my confidence up.

If I'd have failed those first two or three nights, who knows where I'd be today.

And that's the truth.

But thank God, I had success, and that turned everything around, and my confidence grew, and I began feeling like a champion again, feeling like I can achieve, I can do this. And as that confidence grows, you get better and better. Just like I went through a downward spiral, now it was going up.

And I've summarized this demise a little bit, but we all know you don't just end up in the back of a car. I had been spiraling for quite some time and had nothing left to show for it.

I was training more, I was giving more presentations, then the next step was I started teaching others to do what I do, and we all had success together, and it kept growing, and I learned. There's always a learning point, a teachable moment.

Every week that I was out there, I was learning a little bit more about sales, about marketing, about training, about teaching, and then I became an avid reader. It all started though because when you have great success (and I promise you, out of all the people I've trained in sales, the people who aren't with me are usually the ones who had great success their very first month), when you start off great, that's what you think it's always going to be like.

It's like, how many people have been in relationships, and the first two months, it's all just tingly feelings, like, every time you're around them, you hold their hand, or you see them and just get all these tingles?

Well, that ain't love.

It feels like love, it feels good, but that ain't love. You're loving how you feel. You're not thinking about how they feel. You're loving how they make you feel.

But true love is apparent when you see someone who's going through an illness and someone stands by them, and you know at that point, it's in their heart—they love that person. It's not just about how they feel. It's what they can do for that other person.

I saw my mom do that before my father passed away; I saw how much she loved my dad. I always knew she did, but I saw how she stood by him, helped him every day. And so that's where you see true love demonstrated, as opposed to the fake love that lasts about a month or two, then all of a sudden, the little tingly feelings start wearing off, and next thing you know, they've broken up. And you see that happen over and over again.

And so, when you have success too fast, and it comes too easy, it's like that little tingly feeling; it's not really love and it's not really success. You just had a lucky break and a fast start. It's not until you go through a down period that you are truly tested. And hey, this doesn't mean that a fast start isn't amazing. Because it most certainly is. However, what's important is that you stay realistic about it. Next steps are key in sustaining it.

I remember one time when I had set some records in the insurance business, and then this other guy came along, after a couple of years. Where no one had come close to breaking my records, all of a sudden, he started knocking some of them off the board. And I remember telling the owner, I said, "Wow, he's much better than me," and the owner of the company said, "We don't know that, Dennis. We're not gonna know what he's like until he goes through a slow season." And sure enough, a few months down the road, he went through a bad patch and he quit.

And it was obvious what had happened. He had just success, and as long as he was having success, he was there, he was loyal, he was passionate; but as soon as he ran into some negativity, ran into some failures, he gave up.

So for me, being in the backseat of the car, which looked like ultimate failure, turned out to be great success, because when you have success and you win, a championship, let's say, you tend to celebrate. But when you lose, when your back is against the wall and you're down, you don't celebrate, rather you tend to ponder, you tend to think things like, "What can I do to never be here again? How am I going to use this lesson to be my springboard to greatness?"

And when I tend to ponder, for me, when I'm going through periods like that in my life, it's usually what's led to some of the greatest successes. And that is something I can share with people who are going through a down period and saying, "You know, you need to get excited because when you're going through a moment like this, generally it means something big is getting ready to happen, you're getting ready to have a breakthrough. Now, you just need to get prepared for it, get excited and act as if it's going to happen and bring that into your life."

LESSONS LEARNED: Thoughts are things. When you are celebrating a big win, it doesn't guarantee success. If you are sleeping in the back of your car, it doesn't mean you are a failure. You are more than the product of recent results.

Always be on guard to never let your performance slip. Be aware of getting off track, but even if you find yourself off track, you have the ability to turn it around. As the old saying goes, "Tough times don't last, tough people do."

TAKEAWAYS: My experience in what I thought was the low point of my life has turned out to be one of the best learning moments of my career. There have been many other times when I felt the odds were against me, but when I compared them to the backseat of a car, none of them seemed too tough to handle.

If I ever need inspiration, I just remember back to that period of my life and know that I am the same guy who came through that adversity, and that if I keep working hard and working smart and keep my faith in God, I believe I can overcome any situation.

ACTION STEPS: Start to think more "What If" moments.

Start believing bigger in yourself. One of my favorite self-talks that I recite in my head all the time is, "What if I COULD NOT fail, what would I attempt?" If you start applying that kind of mindset, you will be raising the ceiling on what you believe you can achieve.

Maybe it's time to 10X your goals!

Chapter Nineteen

The Million-Dollar Question

When learning from other industries, what we have done in network marketing is to pull together what worked for us in the tanning industry and what worked for us in direct sales. It is the side effect of my having the kind of success I've had in network marketing.

And I say this, even though a lot of what I learned in the industry of network marketing—the importance of making a list, the importance of knowing *why*, giving a presentation, following up with people, and the list goes on—I learned in the network marketing space, but I already knew so much more from traditional business, which I also was able to bring to the table.

For instance, in network marketing, we are taught to do three-way calls. "Okay, John get me on the phone with your buddy Bob, and I'll talk to him," and that's great. But because of my experience in marketing and advertising, I always said, instead of just doing three-way calls, let's do conference calls. Let's have twenty-five people on the line at that time when I'm giving that same presentation as opposed to one person.

Let's leverage it.

Now there may be an occasion when you have a heavy hitter—someone who has a great track record. You want to spend one-on-one time with that person, and that's great. But I would much rather market myself to thirty or forty people at a time instead of one at a time because when I'm advertising with my traditional business, in whatever format it may be, I'm wanting to hit a mass of people.

After that, having narrowed it down to the ones who have interest, I then could spend more time with them. But I am far more interested in leveraging my time and getting myself in front of people who can make a yes or no decision. Because if you go blindly and just one at a time, it can take you while. In fact, it will take you a whole lot longer.

But what you want to do is use your upline, use your company's tools, anything you can do that can shorten the time frame and let you get more exposure faster.

Especially these days, most college or high school grads are going to have eight, ten, twelve jobs in the course of their careers, before they retire. It's not like the old days, when you would go work for one company for the next forty years.

Even if they're in different industries, it doesn't matter, as long as you're learning something and taking it to the next job. I know this, we know this is important because, in my case, in going through direct sales, retail sales, and network marketing sales, all of it made us millions of dollars and success—by using the same principles.

Sure, you'll be learning different strategies, but going across all industries is powerful.

Well, think about it. None of those things were done fast, yet they led me to where I'm at today. Your failures, or what might come before your failures, might be limited success, it might be something you did for five years and now you've moved onto something else.

And that's why, sure, you're learning to make an income, but you're also learning skills that you can use somewhere else. That's part of the whole process.

LESSONS LEARNED: So what is the Million-Dollar Question?

You have something that is more valuable than anything you could purchase in the finest diamond stores in the world. Yet most people treat this valued entity like something off the half-off rack at a flea market.

What is it? Time. In our chase for success, which most people measure in terms of money, many of us do not stop to realize we can always attract and obtain more money. But time is not a renewable resource. When it's gone—we don't get anymore.

So, what is your time worth?

If you knew today that this was your last day on earth and someone had the ability to give you another year, how much would that be worth to you? Would you pay a million dollars for another year with your loved ones? I believe if most people had it, they would gladly spend it for another year with the people they cherish. Yet we all know that life is finite, so many will trade that year of life, or at least a large chunk of it, for an hourly wage.

The Million-Dollar Question is this—How can I get the maximum out of these limited hours I have?

How can I turn twenty-four hours into forty-eight, or ninety-six?

You can do it with leverage, and that is what these business models discussed throughout this book offer you. Wouldn't it be worth your time to make it happen for you? Once I discovered leverage, I felt it was one of the greatest gifts I could ever give myself and my family. This business model(s) not only allowed me to earn incredible income but more importantly—it gave me (us) time-freedom.

TAKEAWAYS: Since we know there is no do-over, and we know that currently, the mortality rate in the world is 100 percent, when should we start to leverage our time? I would suggest NOW!

ACTION STEPS: As the title of this book suggests, *Decide or Drift*, we know when we make a decision, we can now move forward. A better life is usually the result of better decisions. We can leverage what we learn from others and the effects their decisions had on their lives, and learn from their histories to form better decisions for our own lives. The action step you can take right now is to DECIDE. Not another day of drifting and building someone else's dreams.

Decide today to build yours.

Chapter Twenty

Time to Decide

One of my mentors is my father who ran for elective office six times and was beaten six in a row. They actually called him Loser Ligon in the paper because he lost so much, but he stayed at it and then, finally, he won. Then for the next eighteen years, he was in the legislature in North Carolina and he won, gosh, every election from that point on, (obviously) primaries and general elections.

He had a quote that he would use to push me, telling me to take a chance at something, and I'd say "Oh, I'm not going to do that. I can't win." Or whatever.

He said, "Look, when you have very little to lose and a whole lot to gain, by all means, try."

Of course, he said it a little better than that, but it was simply that when there is nothing to lose, or very little to lose, and you've got a great deal to gain, well, go ahead and attempt it. By all means, try. That would be running for office or taking a position or something like that, where the risk is very low.

You might as well give it a try. That's always stuck with me.

And to follow that, one of my favorite quotes I've been using a lot more is, "If your presence doesn't make an impact, your absence won't make a difference."

Getting in, especially in the network marketing business, and trying to make an impact, and doing the things that move the needle, that bring dollars in the door, and moving product, these are the income-producing activities. Everything else is just fluff.

We always talk about aggressively getting ready to start. People sit in that mode of just studying and aggressively getting ready, but they never get started.

Some of the mentors I've always looked up to are, you know, big-time coaches like Vince Lombardi; been a Green Bay Packers fan all my life, and of course, there are all the quotes of Vince Lombardi, how he just took average, ordinary people and turned them into champions. I loved Bear Bryant with Alabama, where they used to say he could take his eleven players to beat you, then he could take your eleven players and beat you again. In other words, he just believed in fundamentals. A lot of these great coaches in the past were just getting the fundamentals right over and over and doing things over and over, until they were to perfection, rather than learning something new.

That's what happens in network marketing. So many people want to give me something new; I've heard that before. But yet, they've never learned the basics. John Wooden, the greatest coach of all time in basketball, won, I think, twelve national championships in fourteen years, including eight or nine in a row. That'll never be repeated. His first practice was teaching people how to tie their tennis shoes. It was always the basics, getting people to get and to learn to love the basics, the fundamentals, and appreciate that structure that would lead to success.

That's why what lead to getting this book going is that I quickly realized that I did not have the structure to stay on this and get it done, and that I was just drifting along. This book could have taken years to write, if ever got written, and that is the truth.

Having the knowledge to take a bunch of jibber-jabber and put it all together, and structure it, and make it all come together in a format is not a strength for me. This is a blessing to be able to have someone pull it together. Let's face it, the first two months, I was in this book-writing program, and I was getting rolling, when the person supporting me . . . quit. Then, I was moved to somebody else for support, and I had to start all over. And I'm happy I did—with the right support.

There was a gentleman by the name of John Locke, who was the first person to really impact me in the world of business. He was in the insurance business, and although I've lost track of him now, I recall there was one thing he would always say, "Do you know who the best manager is we have in this industry?" I'm sitting there and have no idea who he's talking about. He was pointing to me, and it blew my mind because I had never even thought of myself as that good, but here was somebody who lifted me up. He was one of the first people who made me believe more in myself. He believed in me more than I believed in myself, and started me down that road of thinking maybe I can be better than I'd thought I could be.

Along the way, there have been a lot of leaders who have lifted me up. In the network marketing world, there was Ruth Elliot. Ruth noticed that I was having some success, and she immediately reached out and spent the next year working with me and helping me rank advance through the company. She connected me to another great mentor, BK Boreyko, who was the CEO of the firm, and together, they continued to breathe life into my dream. Then, there was Ryan Anderson, who was probably for me the closest embodiment of my father in believing the best in people. I love the way he combines passion with purpose, and I have learned so much in just a few years. Along the way, in different industries and businesses, I have truly learned the power of lifting people up. Something I've learned, and that's what I want to do during the rest of my years in business actually, is to make it a conscious effort to lift people up, especially people getting started, to know the encouragement that can make a big difference.

Others have mentored me, without knowing it, by their examples. My mom said to do what you are expected to do, but she always had grace when I fell short. She, to me, is the greatest example of living the

Christian life that I have known, and for that I owe her everything. My son, Josh, has excelled at sports and cultivating friendships. Whereas, I was shy growing up, I've seen in my son the value of putting yourself out there in sports and friendships, risking rejection but cultivating a lot of experiences along the way. My daughter, Jordan—who has shown me persistence and has the most loving heart for people— tackled college on her own and has excelled, far outpacing anything I ever did in higher education. But she does it all with a humble, caring heart. She shows that nice people can finish first. Finally, it goes without saying my wife, Sue, has been my rock. Through seven years of marriage, she has supported my dreams while following her own.

Whenever I have any self-doubt, Sue is the one person I know who can get me back on track. We met through a network marketing business that had a pay plan containing a lot of bonuses. Once, when speaking from stage, I referred to Sue as the greatest bonus the company ever offered, and they offered it only one time—and I was the beneficiary of the "blonde bonus." Although the line got a laugh from the 8,000 in the audience, in truth, Sue is more a gift from God. I am thankful every day that our paths crossed, and that we get to do this thing called life together.

There's plenty of other people who are going to give people starting out the structure in terms of discipline, but my role through this book, through websites, through coaching, and speaking will always be to lift them up and make them feel like they can accomplish big things.

You never know until you try, and you will surprise yourself.

These are the things I want to pass onto you—primarily, because they have literally moved me.

Would this book be complete without referencing the five people you hang around? I heard that years ago, and it didn't really stick with me until recently when I realized their impact in my life. That's what really moved me forward, getting to the people I hang around, the people who inspire me.

Life is a moving parade. I use this phrase a lot because somebody may not have any interest in what you're talking about today, but their life could be totally different a month from now. I think about the vice president of sales of my company, Erica Soltys. When Erica found out she was pregnant, all of a sudden she started noticing things associated with a newborn; things she would have never thought about before were now very important. I told her, "You're noticing car seats, baby clothes—now you're noticing all baby-type stuff you didn't even look at year ago." Life truly is a moving parade.

When life changes, it can change the person you're talking to, their interest in what you're offering. For sales, I always say, "Because they say no today doesn't mean they're going to be saying no a month from now." I constantly realize how life is a moving parade and things are changing.

I hope that from this moment on, you will enjoy your moving parade.

You deserve it.

26660883R00066

Made in the USA
San Bernardino, CA
21 February 2019